ISLAND WINERIES OF BRITISH COLUMBIA

ISLAND WINERIES

OF BRITISH COLUMBIA

From the contributors of *EAT Magazine*
Edited by Gary Hynes
Photography by Rebecca Wellman

TouchWood
Editions

TouchWood Editions
www.touchwoodeditions.com

Library and Archives Canada Cataloguing in Publication
Island wineries of British Columbia / [edited by] Gary Hynes.

Includes index.
Print format: ISBN 978-1-926741-26-0
Electronic monograph in PDF format: ISBN 978-1-926741-27-7

1. Wineries—British Columbia—Guidebooks. 2. Wine and wine making—British Columbia. I. Hynes, Gary

TP559.C3W56 2011   663'.2009711   C2010-907497-1

Editor: Marlyn Horsdal
Proofreader: Holland Gidney
Design: Pete Kohut
Cover image: Rebecca Wellman
All images can be credited to Rebecca Wellman Photography.
Other photos credited as follows: page 5 Image I-04374 Courtesy of Royal BC Museum, BC Archives; page 110 Gary Hynes; page 112 Norman Eder, istockphoto.com; page 120 Gary Hynes; page 123 John Shepherd, istockphoto.com; page 126 Paul Troop; page 129 Božo Kodrič, istockphoto.com; page 132 Palle Christensen, istockphoto.com; page 136 Florin Tirlea, istockphoto.com; page 141 left Gary Hynes; page 146 Ferran Trainte Soler, istockphoto.com; page 150 Sara Gray, istockphoto.com; page 158 Michael Sloneck, stck.xchng; Ben Earwicker, stck.xchng; page 202 Steve Cole, istockphoto.com; page 207 Liang Zhang, istockphoto.com; page 210 Stephen Walls, istockphoto.com.

We gratefully acknowledge the financial support for our publishing activities from the Government of Canada through the Canada Book Fund, Canada Council for the Arts, and the province of British Columbia through the British Columbia Arts Council and the Book Publishing Tax Credit.

This book was produced using FSC-certified, acid-free paper, processed chlorine free, and printed with vegetable-based inks.

The information in this book is true and complete to the best of the author's knowledge. All recommendations are made without guarantee on the part of the author. The author disclaims any liability in connection with the use of this information.

1 2 3 4 5 14 13 12 11

For my wife, Cynthia, and son, Colin.

VANCOUVER ISLAND AND GULF ISLANDS

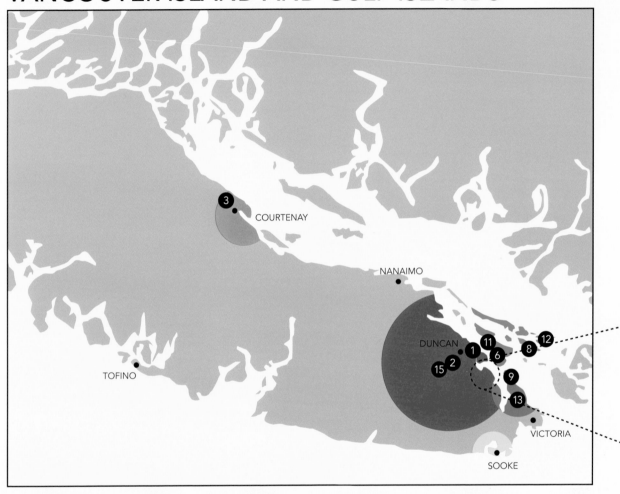

COURTENAY

NANAIMO

DUNCAN

TOFINO

VICTORIA

SOOKE

1 Alderlea Vineyards

2 Averill Creek Vineyard

3 Beaufort Winery Vineyard
    & Estate Winery

4 Blue Grouse Vineyards & Winery

5 Cherry Point Estate Wines

6 Garry Oaks Winery

7 Glenterra Vineyards

8 Morning Bay Vineyard
    & Estate Winery

9 Muse Winery

10 Rocky Creek Winery

11 Salt Spring Vineyards

12 Saturna Island Family
     Estate Winery

13 Starling Lane Winery

14 Venturi-Schulze Vineyards

15 Vigneti Zanatta

CONTENTS

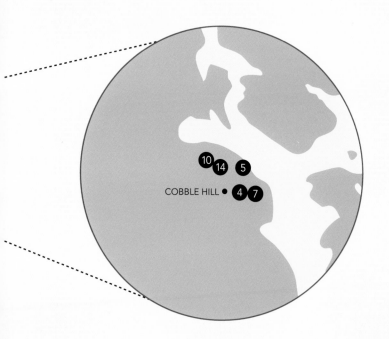

COBBLE HILL

The maps included in this book are not for navigational purposes, please use a road map when planning your trip. The information on each of the businesses profiled here is accurate to the best of the editor's knowledge at the time of this going to press. For more information contact the business directly or visit their website.

EDITOR'S INTRODUCTION

Gary Hynes

This book, *Island Wineries of British Columbia*, provides an introduction to the growing number of wineries on Vancouver Island and the surrounding Gulf Islands—a celebration, too, of the unique flavours, *terroir,* and grape varieties found here. It is a collaborative effort by the writers at *EAT Magazine*, with each writer bringing a particular expertise and point of view to create a book that will inspire you to explore this new and developing wine region and its wines.

The book opens with an overview of the history of the wine industry on the islands. Ours is an extremely young wine region and the stories are about the pioneers: tales of tenacious perseverance and overcoming the challenges of a cool-climate wine region on the fringe of the grape-growing world. Imagine having to carve a vineyard out of dense fir forest while keeping the black bears at bay!

What do you need to know to enjoy these wines? You need to know the wineries, what wines they produce, and where the wineries can be found. Did you know there are over 25 wineries to explore? We have scaled back much of the heavy technical information so don't think you need to take a course before reading this book. We interviewed the winemakers and it's their stories you'll be reading. If nothing else, this book will enable you to visit your local wine shop and quickly pick out bottles to take home and savour.

In the second part of the book we examine the locally grown grape varieties— many new and unfamiliar—that you will encounter. With our coastal, northern location, winemakers have planted grape varieties to match our soils and climate, enabling them to craft the finest wines that can be produced here. Our style is very different from California, Australia, and even BC's Okanagan Valley; crisp, aromatic whites and lighter, cool-climate reds are the best possible expression of our region. We also note a few of the signature styles that are particularly well suited for our area—most notably sparkling wine (or "bubble," as I like to call it), blackberry dessert wines, and an up-and-coming group of wines with an odd-sounding name (Blattner anyone?).

Our region has more than wine alone. You will also find sections on meaderies, cideries, fruit wineries, craft breweries, and artisan distilleries—in fact a whole world of alcoholic beverages is made on our doorstep.

Of course, wine is meant to be enjoyed with good food. Wine enhances food and food brings out the best qualities of a wine. Vancouver Island and the Gulf Islands are known for excellent meats, seafood, fruits, and vegetables. So we asked a select group of chefs from local restaurants if they would create recipes that were island wine-friendly. We picked these restaurants for the support they give the local wine industry, and the chefs were definitely up to the task as you will see from the broad range of seasonal recipes they provided. These recipes can easily be cooked at home and appreciated with the wines we suggest to go with them. I call it a delicious kitchen tour of island wines and foods.

Speaking of tours, the last chapter in the book offers our suggested wine-touring excursions. We break down the region into separate, manageable sips, with tours that can be taken as a single day trip or strung together for a longer trip. We note the tasting rooms, highway turns, restaurant and café stops, picnic locations, and more.

Island Wineries of British Columbia is not meant to be an academic tome nor the last word on the subject. My hope is that it will serve as an introduction, for both locals and visitors, to the many wonderful wines and the people who make them; to inspire you to go out into the countryside and tour the wineries, taste the wines, and meet the winemakers. Use this book as a first-step guide to discovering the best of Vancouver Island and Gulf Islands wines.

Cheers!

VANCOUVER ISLAND

Born of Fire, Scoured by Ice!—The History of the Island's Wines

Larry Arnold

Born of fire, scoured by ice, Vancouver Island lies on the eastern mantle of the Pacific Ring of Fire. Running north to south, the island forms the southwest corner of the province of British Columbia, Canada. It is 460 kilometres in length but only 50 kilometres at its widest point and is divided down the middle by the Vancouver Island Ranges. The west side of the range, facing the vast expanse of the Pacific Ocean, is rugged, wet, and densely forested, with stands of old-growth cedar, hemlock, and fir still to be found. A lovely place to visit but most islanders prefer the milder and drier climate of the southeast coast of the island.

Here, in the rain shadow of the island's looming mountain range, the climate throughout the year is mild, with all manner of plants and trees in bloom and the mercury often in the teens (Celsius) throughout the coldest winter months. Since southern Vancouver Island is blessed with the warmest median temperature in Canada, dry summers, and much arable land suitable for grape growing, it is not difficult to envision a thriving wine industry here.

It is a beautiful dream, yet although the lion's share of island vineyards are located just south of the 49th parallel, they are still located at the northern extreme of world grape production. The growing season at this latitude is very short; however, what it lacks in days it makes back in hours. With long warm days and short cool nights, good science, and a lot of luck, wines of great finesse and varietal character are more than just a possibility; they are a common occurrence.

Although Vancouver Island has a long, colourful history of wine production, boasting several of the first wineries in the province, it does not have a long history of commercial grape production. The original wine industry was not based on grapes but on other locally grown fruit, in particular, the loganberry. The industry as we know it today is only a couple of decades young with the inspiration to grow grapes on Vancouver Island initially conceived by the provincial government.

Prior to the North American Free Trade Agreement (NAFTA) in 1988 and the General Agreement on Tariffs and Trade (GATT) in 1989, the BC wine industry was an uneasy partnership of wineries and grape growers based in the Okanagan Valley and protected from outside competition by a wall of preferential pricing mechanisms. In the late 1980s, Canada committed itself to gradually phasing out discriminatory trade practices. A howl of protest from the vinous hinterland reverberated across the land, proclaiming financial ruin if something wasn't done to right this wrong.

The major problem was that the BC wine industry was located at the northern climatic extreme for growing and ripening grapes, and it was a commonly held belief that the severity of Canadian winters would put an end to all but the heartiest varieties. Unfortunately, the heartiest, while perfectly acceptable for the production of fortified dessert wines or Fuddle Duck, a sweet, sparkling wine, are somewhat lacking when it comes to producing high-quality, dry table wines. To compete with newly arrived, low-cost wine imports, the first order of business was to replant existing vineyards with vines capable of producing high-quality grapes, yet also of surviving the dreaded Canadian winter. The solution was the Grape and Wine Sector Adjustment Program. Twenty-eight million dollars was allocated to helping growers replant their vineyards with high-quality *vinifera* vines. The problem then became finding enough plant material to meet the demand. At this point, European nurseries were the major suppliers of plant material and they couldn't come up with the goods. The answer was to produce tissue cultures from plant material sourced from local vineyards.

With this in mind, a government study was initiated in 1983 to determine if wine and table grapes could be grown successfully in the maritime climate of Vancouver Island. The initial test vineyard was a one-acre site on the Zanatta farm, just outside the city of Duncan in the Cowichan Valley. Sixty-one grape varieties were planted

Harvesting grapes on the Saanich Peninsula on Vancouver Island in 1978.

over a four-year period for assessment, and, although the project was terminated in 1990 when government funding ran out, the results of the study were promising, if somewhat inconclusive. Shortly after the Duncan Project ended, a second island vineyard was planted, by famed British Columbia orchardist John Harper at what is now Blue Grouse Vineyards. This new private enterprise soon ran into financial difficulties and was eventually sold to its present owner, Dr. Hans Kiltz.

In the fall of 1992, Vigneti Zanatta opened its doors to the public, becoming the first farm-gate winery on Vancouver Island. They had only one wine to sell, a 1991 Ortega, and were sold out by Christmas. Today, there are over 30 wine, cider, and mead producers on Vancouver Island, with many more on the way.

The interior and coastal wine regions of BC are vastly different. The desert-like Okanagan and Similkameen valleys are semi-arid, with extreme temperature variations both diurnally and seasonally. Vines there must be able to survive long, cold winters and still be capable of producing ripe fruit in a relatively short growing season. Long hours of bright sunlight, warm temperatures, and access to an abundance of water allow this to happen.

The vineyards of Vancouver Island and the Gulf Islands, because of their proximity to the moderating influence of the Pacific Ocean, have a warmer median temperature, do not experience the extreme spikes in temperature, and are slightly wetter.

Bud break (when the first shoots emerge on a vine after winter dormancy) starts earlier on the coast but, because of the vast difference in temperature, it is not long before Okanagan fruit has caught up and surpassed the island in the race to maturity. Herein lies a major reason for the stylistic difference between the two regions: Interior fruit matures faster; coastal fruit requires a longer growing season to ripen. It is this extended hang time that enables island vines to produce wines of outstanding delicacy and balance, with rich fruit character and soft acidity. Both regions have the potential to produce wines of sublime quality, showing pronounced varietal characteristics specific to their own unique *terroir*.

The wine industry on the islands has steadily expanded since its humble beginnings in the fall of 1992 but it is small and family owned. Vintners of Europe learned their lessons over centuries of trial and error but growers toiling in the vineyards of Vancouver Island do not have the luxury of collective knowledge gleaned in the fields through the generations. Island vintners are still learning about what to plant and where. Though the island industry is still very much in its infancy and is learning as it goes along, one thing it has certainly learned is how to make better, cleaner, more interesting wines than it did a few short years ago.

A basic rule of thumb is that it takes 100 days after flowering for grapes to ripen. On Vancouver Island, it takes between 120 and 150 days to fully ripen grapes. Given the nature of the local climate, the industry is never going to have an easy go of it. Over a given period of time there will probably be more difficult vintages than good. As in many other winemaking regions, it will be good decisions made in the vineyard rather than state-of-the-art equipment in the winery that will ultimately determine the success of Vancouver Island and the Gulf Islands as a wine region.

Wine Making on Vancouver Island

Although the industry as we know it today has only been around for a couple of decades, commercial wine production on Vancouver Island has a long and illustrious history. First out of the gate in British Columbia, after the repeal of Prohibition in 1920, was the Growers Wine Cooperative of Victoria. In the beginning, Growers used locally grown loganberries to produce sweet fruit wines, but by the mid-1930s the company had started making a wide range of sweet wines from Okanagan-grown Lambrusco grapes. Growers Wine, under its company motto,

"What western Canada makes, makes western Canada," pioneered many successful provincial brands, including Logana, Vin Supreme, and Slingers. In 1973, Growers Wine, which had merged with Victoria Wineries and changed its name to Castle Wines, was acquired by the Ontario-based giant Jordan Wines and was renamed Jordan & Ste-Michelle the following year. Production was finally shut down at the old winery in Victoria in 1978 and moved to Surrey, on the mainland, thus ending 57 years of commercial wine production on Vancouver Island.

In late summer, Cabernet Libre grapes hang heavy on the vines in the Cowichan Valley. The Cowichan's long, Mediterranean-like growing season and mild, maritime winters make it the most important agricultural area on Vancouver Island.

THE WINERIES

A late summer afternoon at Cherry Point Estate Wines, located in the Cowichan Valley on Vancouver Island. The vineyard was planted on the side of a stony, glacial moraine hill.

INTRODUCTION

Island Wine on Island Time

Adem Tepedelen

In wine years, Vancouver Island and Gulf Islands vineyards are still in their infancy. Though grapes have been grown here and wine made commercially in the Designated Viticultural Area (DVA) appellations since the late 1980s and early '90s, much about the land and climate is still being discovered. What has been quite clearly established, though, is that this is a region best suited to cooler-climate varietals, and, for the most part, that eliminates Cabernet Sauvignon, Merlot, Syrah, and other black grapes that thrive in hot weather and ripen late in the season.

But that doesn't mean great red wines aren't made here. Pinot Noir does wonderfully in the warmth of the Cowichan Valley, and early-ripening hybrids such as Marechal Foch have also been grown to make big, fruit-forward reds of great stature. Some vintners are even having success with Merlot.

Latitude-wise, the islands are roughly in line with northern France and central Germany. Not surprisingly, many of the varietals that have thus far thrived here—Pinot Gris, Bacchus, Ortega, Siegerrebe, Müller-Thurgau, Pinot Noir, Pinot Auxerrois, and Gewürztraminer—are from, or are crosses of grapes from, that area. There's also much potential for making high-quality sparkling wine, which, depending on the style, doesn't necessarily mean that grapes have to attain the same level of ripeness as table wine.

There are challenges here, and limitations, too, but for winemakers willing to take advantage of the positives—mild winters, proper soil, and warm summers—wine that reflects the true character of this region, its *terroir*, can be made. Each of the wineries described here is discovering, and perhaps establishing, the true taste of Vancouver Island and Gulf Islands wine.

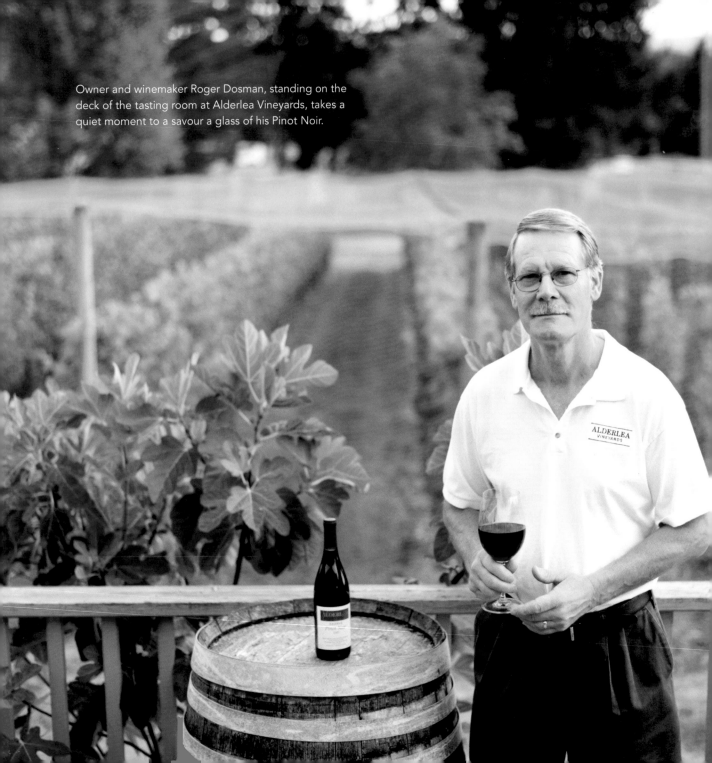

Owner and winemaker Roger Dosman, standing on the deck of the tasting room at Alderlea Vineyards, takes a quiet moment to a savour a glass of his Pinot Noir.

ALDERLEA VINEYARDS

Sitting on the porch of what was once an old barn but which now houses Alderlea Vineyards' small, simple tasting room and winemaking facility, you can pretty much see all the factors that conspire to make its wines consistently good. There is a gentle slope to this south-facing Cowichan Valley property, providing proper drainage for the eight acres of vines that surround the building. Off to the southeast, you can see Mount Tzouhalem, a 536-metre sentinel that helps protect the vineyard from cool marine air off the Strait of Georgia. And even on a cloudy spring morning, with the bright-green buds of new growth just starting to erupt along the rough-looking vines, it's still easy to imagine the copious amount of sunshine the grapes will soak up during the long summer days.

Alderlea is owned and run by winemaker Roger Dosman and his wife, Nancy. It's a small operation that produces, at maximum capacity, about 2,000 cases of estate-grown wine in a good year. That means that every drop of wine that leaves this ten-acre farm, just northeast of Duncan, comes from the grapes nurtured and tended by the Dosmans. They need only step out the back door of their house,

positioned at the front of the property by the road, to see the entirety of their vineyard stretching up the hill.

They bought the property and cleared the trees off in 1992, let the land rest for the whole of 1993, and then planted their first vines, some Bacchus, in 1994. Subsequent years saw plantings of Auxerrois, Pinot Noir, Pinot Gris, Marechal Foch, Gewürztraminer, Chardonnay, Merlot, and "all kinds of silly stuff," according to Dosman. "We've probably planted 30 or 40 varieties over the years, just to see what works and what doesn't."

Not surprisingly, ten vintages later, he's still trying, to some degree, to figure that out. Though much of the "silly stuff" has since been pulled, in a normal year Dosman will bottle up to ten different wines. The whites include Bacchus, a Chardonnay/Auxerrois blend, Pinot Gris, and occasionally Gewürztraminer and Viognier. The reds make up more than half of his production and include two Pinot Noirs (a reserve and a "regular"), Merlot, Clarinet (Marechal Foch), Heritage Hearth (port-style), and their newest release, Fusion, made from a Cabernet Sauvignon/Marechal Foch hybrid created by Swiss plant breeder Valentin Blattner.

Dosman started experimenting with ten different Blattner hybrids eight years ago—mostly reds—and thinks that they may well be the future of red wine on Vancouver Island and the Gulf Islands. "Not only do they make great wine,"

Best Vintages: 2000, 2002–2007, 2009
(with 2006 a particular stand-out)

Open to the Public: Yes (call for hours)

1751 Stamps Road
Duncan
T: 250-746-7122
W: alderlea.com

he says, "but they are also very resistant to diseases like powdery mildew and botrytis. Most of the [Blattner hybrids] have a Cabernet Sauvignon base, which is why they produce more of a warmer climate-structured wine. Here you have this big, fat, juicy, well-structured, really nice-tannined wine from a cool climate."

In a cool-climate region like Vancouver Island, winemakers have to be more tuned into what the land, the weather, and the climate will let them do. Yes, their options may be more limited, but winemakers like Dosman, who accept and acknowledge this, instead of trying to defy it, are learning that some truly remarkable wines can be made here. And in those wines—whether they are Pinot Gris or Marechal Foch—the true taste, the *terroir*, of the island will reveal itself, something Dosman is already seeing in his own vineyard. "I can say that after ten vintages there seems to be something here through all different weather patterns and seasons. I think through all of our reds there's a vein of an allspice character. Most are grown up in the lighter, gravelly soils, and there's an absolute character of wine there. Not only from year to year, but from wine to wine. Certainly Pinot Noir and Merlot have different flavours from the Foch, but there is a flavour that's almost a structure that's quite unique to us."

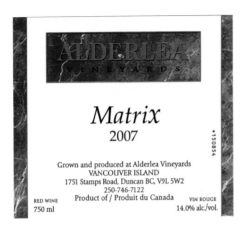

ALDERLEA
V I N E Y A R D S

Matrix
2007

+150854

Grown and produced at Alderlea Vineyards
VANCOUVER ISLAND
1751 Stamps Road, Duncan BC, V9L 5W2
250-746-7122
Product of / Produit du Canada

RED WINE
750 ml

VIN ROUGE
14.0% alc./vol.

The deck of the Alderlea Vineyards' tasting room overlooks the vineyard, which is covered with blue netting designed to keep the birds from stealing the harvest. In the foreground are fig trees, a common sight in many island vineyards.

Averill Creek owner Andy Johnston spends most of his days in the vineyard—pictured here in full-leaf midway into the grape-growing season—examining the progress and health of the ripening grapes.

AVERILL CREEK VINEYARD

One of Vancouver Island's newer winemakers, Averill Creek Vineyard owner Andy Johnston is also one of the biggest proponents of the great wine made here. While other island wineries have been almost apologetic about being based here, augmenting their estate-grown offerings with wines made from Okanagan grapes, he proudly trumpets his estate-grown selection and uses nothing but grapes grown on his nearly 30-acre Cowichan Valley vineyard on Mount Prevost, northwest of Duncan.

"I think the future of [the Vancouver Island wine] industry has to be based on growing our own grapes and creating our own identity," he proudly states. "For me, the only way you can go that makes any kind of business sense is to grow your grapes, make your wine. I'm really quite militant about that."

Johnston, a physician and one of the founders of Medicentres, the first primary-care walk-in centres in Canada, is truly putting his money where his mouth is in this regard. Since purchasing the land in 2001, he has spared no effort to do things right—from taking great pains to prep the land for vines to putting in a top-quality,

gravity-fed winery. "I did go in with a very solid business plan," he says, "with my own independent funding. That's crucial. A lot of people have come into it bit by bit and that's a very difficult way to go."

But Johnston didn't come to Vancouver Island with simply a business plan. He brought a passion for wine fostered by numerous stints working in wineries in France, Italy, New Zealand, and Australia where he honed his viniculture and viticulture skills along the way. Though he initially looked into starting a winery in the Okanagan, the Cowichan Valley, as it turns out, was a much better fit all around. "This was to me a brand-new oenological area which had incredible potential, and the land was cheap. In the Okanagan, you're looking at $30,000 to $70,000 dollars an acre and you can't find good acreage anymore. My land was $7,000 an acre."

Averill Creek's first harvest in 2004—on his original 15-acre vineyard— was a scant seven tonnes of Pinot Noir, Pinot Gris, a little bit of Merlot and Gewürztraminer. The following year, he planted Marechal Foch and a Marechal Foch/Cabernet Sauvignon hybrid (one of the Blattner varieties that Roger Dosman at Alderlea is also very enthusiastic about). That same year, he upped his acreage under vine to 29. In the ensuing vintages, both the quality and the quantity have continually improved as the vines have matured. In the October 2009 harvest,

Best Vintages: 2005, 2006 and 2009
(a great year in the Cowichan Valley with a
long, hot and dry summer.)

Open to the Public: Yes
(check website for hours)

6552 North Road
Duncan
T: 250-709-9986
E: andyj@averillcreek.ca
W: averillcreek.ca

those 29 acres yielded a whopping 85 tonnes of "top-quality product," 22 tonnes of which were Pinot Noir. "We're going to be making 1,500 cases of top-end Pinot Noir for release in 2011," he says, with no small amount of pride. "We've really come a long way."

Johnston's estimated Pinot Noir production for 2011 comes close to rivalling the total production of some of his well-established neighbours who, of course, have many fewer acres under vine. "We're certainly, by far, the biggest [in the Cowichan Valley]," he says. "There's nobody close as far as the volume of product we're actually growing." And as the vines continue to mature and his own skills in vineyard management continue to improve, Johnston anticipates the steep increase in production to continue. "We had 3,800 cases for sale in 2009," he explains. "Next year we'll be 5,000-plus; in 2011 we'll be 7,000-plus, and [we may] push the 10,000-case mark within three to five years."

Though he's only been making wine on Vancouver Island for six years, Johnston believes not only that there is great potential here but that part of that potential lies in the fact that there is an identifiable Vancouver Island profile to be found in the locally made wines, particularly the Pinot Noirs. "There is a strong Cowichan Valley Pinot Noir identity, which is a very pronounced black cherry flavour," he posits. "You can see this in Roger Dosman's, mine, Venturi-Schulze, Blue Grouse. You can

pick [these wines] out in a tasting and know [they're] Cowichan Valley Pinot Noir. I think that's very exciting for us to have that kind of identity."

Johnston intends to do his part to help increase the region's prominence. The first few vintages of his Pinot Noir have been well received and he has, accordingly, set his sights high for what he hopes to achieve. "Simply the best Pinot Noir in Canada. For me, that's my goal, and I think we're well on our way to doing it now. There's a lovely progression through our Pinot Noirs from 2004 to 2008 and you can see the wine developing as the vines get older. We will be making some of the best Pinot Noirs in Canada on this site. There's no question in my mind about that. It's my raison d'être."

Situated northwest of Duncan, Averill Creek Vineyard enjoys a spectacular view over the fertile, rolling hills of the Cowichan Valley.

Beaufort Winery Vineyard and Estate Winery owners/winemakers Susan and Jeff Vandermolen share a moment beside their "mascot," a towering, Easter Island-inspired wood carving. This beautiful carving appears on many of their wine labels.

BEAUFORT WINERY VINEYARD & ESTATE WINERY

It's all about location, location, location when it comes to starting a new winery on Vancouver Island. Susan and Jeff Vandermolen knew they wanted to do something agricultural in the Comox Valley, but they weren't entirely sure they could successfully grow quality wine grapes there. It would ultimately hinge on whether they could find the right spot. "We met with our regional agrologist, Jill Hatfield, and gave her the guidelines of what we were looking for and she just kept pointing to this ridge that we're on called Ransom Ridge," explains Jeff, Beaufort's vineyard manager. "[The property] was bigger than we were planning on, but it's ideal. It has a nice gentle slope, it's all south-facing, and all the rows are oriented to the south and full-on exposure east to west. It's about as good as you can get."

The couple found their perfect spot—85 acres with a view of the Beaufort Mountain range to the west, hence the winery's name—at the end of 2005 and began planting eight acres of cool-climate white grapes like Ortega, Siegerrebe, Pinot Gris, and Schonburger, as well as the hybrid red Marechal Foch and its cousin, Leon Millot. "We're predominantly red wine lovers," says Jeff, "so we

wanted at least two-thirds of the vineyard to be red wine grapes. In the cool climate, that's a bit of a challenge. It really narrows down the field [as far as what you can grow]." And, like other island vintners dedicated to estate-made wines, and trying to meet public demand for big, full-bodied red wines, the Vandermolens were ultimately led to put in 900 Blattner hybrid vines in 2007.

Beaufort's first vintages—starting with a meagre two tonnes of Gewürztraminer pressed in 2006 were mostly made from grapes grown on the island, though they did (and will continue to do so in the future) buy some Okanagan grapes for specific offerings such as their Cabernet Sauvignon. Their timing for starting a winery, however, was rather unfortunate. The 2007 and 2008 vintages were trying for all island winemakers and a true test for winemaker Susan Vandermolen, a chemical engineer by trade and long-time winemaking hobbyist. "We opened the tasting room in the spring of 2008," says Jeff, "and it was a bit of a nervous time for us, because we had marginal grapes from the '07 vintage. But we [entered] a few wines in a couple of competitions and came away with some medals and I think that kind of gave us a lot of confidence—that, in a marginal year, we can actually make good wines."

And though they are just a few vintages into their winemaking adventures on the island, they already have an appreciation of what makes this such a unique wine

Best Vintages: 2009

Open to the Public: Yes
(check website for hours)

5854 Pickering Road
Courtenay
T: 250-338-1357
E: beaufortwines@shaw.ca
W: beaufortwines.ca

region, especially when it comes to one of the more prominent and popular grapes. "The beauty of Pinot Gris on Vancouver Island," says Jeff, "is that high acidity and low brix [a measurement of the amount of sugar in a liquid] are not necessarily a bad thing. Those are the characteristics that almost identify the region—that crisp acidity."

Luckily, the 2009 vintage turned out to be a good one—the kind that makes winemaking seem easy—and it came when the couple undertook the first harvest of their own grapes. "We're really excited about this vintage," enthuses Jeff. "We were able to pull off a small but high-quality crop from our own estate. This is the first year when we are actually making wine from our estate grapes, so that's pretty exciting. We've got high hopes for this vintage."

Now that their own vineyard is maturing, the Vandermolens will start to approach their projected production capacity. "Our business plan has always been to produce between 1,800 and 2,000 cases per year," says Jeff. "I think we'll probably split that fifty-fifty between reds and whites. And we'll probably produce about 1,200 cases from our estate-grown grapes." The other 600 or so cases will be made from Okanagan grapes to, as Jeff explains, "keep things interesting—we love to make wines from noble red grapes like Cab Sauv, Malbec, Syrah—and for risk management, in case we have a disastrous year [on the island]."

Sparkling Pinot Noir - Traditional Method
VANCOUVER ISLAND / ÎLE de VANCOUVER
Red Wine / Vin Rouge
12.5% alc./vol.   750 ml

The Vandermolens have come to accept and understand that even finding the perfect location for a winery comes with other challenges, namely the hard work of farming that land to grow the grapes that your livelihood depends on. "If there's one thing that I would caution anyone with romance in their eyes about this business," says Jeff, "it's that it's a helluva lot of work. When the grapes need your attention, you've gotta go out and do it, regardless of how you feel. We've had lots of long days and many hours in the vineyard, but it's also very rewarding. There are few things nicer than being out in the vineyard amongst the grapes, trimming. It's a good place to be."

View from the public picnic area at Beaufort Winery in the Comox Valley. Vineyards surround this peaceful spot. The family lives on the estate and their home is pictured.

Hans Kiltz, Blue Grouse Vineyards & Winery owner and winemaker, is one of the early pioneers who built and shaped the wine industry on Vancouver Island.

BLUE GROUSE
VINEYARDS & WINERY

Making sacrifices is a necessary part of crafting high-quality wine on Vancouver Island. And no one understands that better than Blue Grouse patriarch/senior winemaker Hans Kiltz, who brought his family—wife Evangeline, son Richard and daughter Sandrina—to the Cowichan Valley in 1988 and purchased a 31-acre plot southwest of Duncan that included an experimental vineyard.

Though there were some 156 different varieties being propagated in that one-acre vineyard, he set out zeroing in on the ones he knew would do well and clearing an additional nine acres to plant varieties well-suited to the short, volatile growing season. "The basic thought here is that we have a climate similar to the moderate wine regions of Europe, like Germany, Austria, and Switzerland," he says. "And the wine industry in Germany is mainly based on Riesling varieties."

Kiltz, a Berlin native himself, knows European wines and the challenges of growing *vinifera* grapes in cool climates, so he took the path of least resistance and sought to follow the European model, with initially mixed results. "We tried

growing Riesling here, but it's not the same. I wasn't happy with it so I pulled it out. What are doing much better are Riesling crosses."

Which was one of a succession of sacrifices he had to make along the way. As juicy, crisp, and delicious as these Riesling crosses are—and Blue Grouse's are superlative—they do not come with the same cachet as the noble grape varieties. But Kiltz knew he could make good wine with them. So in the late 1980s—long before any Vancouver Island wineries except Vigneti Zanatta existed—in went Bacchus, Müller-Thurgau, Ortega, and Siegerrebe, all early-ripening Riesling crosses. Unfortunately, these names didn't initially register with North Americans who have only in the past 40 years come around to fine wine. "It's difficult to market a variety that's not well known. I had this problem with the Ortega at the beginning because it sounds Spanish, but it's a German grape."

At least one of his early plantings, as it turns out, wasn't such a hard sell and has become one of Blue Grouse's most highly regarded wines. Their Pinot Gris, a classic Alsatian varietal, is like a tropical fruit basket in the mouth. Full of juicy, ripe flavours, it also has a nice, slightly pink hue—a testament to the ripeness Kiltz can attain on his sunny, south-facing vineyard.

That abundant sunshine also helps develop the red wines—Pinot Noir, Gamay Noir, and the unique Black Muscat—that Kiltz eventually added to his lineup,

Best Vintages: 2001–2006, 2009

Open to the Public: Yes
(check website for hours)

4365 Blue Grouse Road
Duncan
T: 250-743-3834
E: info@bluegrousevineyards.com
W: bluegrousevineyards.com

something they didn't plan on 20 years ago. "I was reluctant to plant red varieties at the very beginning," Kiltz admits, "but the demand is there."

To make such high-quality wines and be successful year in and year out, however, has meant continued concessions to the island climate. One of the greatest is accepting that to maintain quality, they must sometimes significantly sacrifice yield. Some years they can produce 3,000 cases, others may net only 1,600. The last two vintages have been particularly challenging due to poor weather, but the smaller quantities weren't diminished in quality due to their selectivity in the vineyard. "[In poor years] you have a smaller [yield]," explains Kiltz, "because you crop back as much as you can and lose grapes because you decide not to pick them because they're not properly ripened. Last year, we left about 50 percent of the Pinot Gris out there. We picked the ones we thought were ripe enough."

So these are the sacrifices Vancouver Island wineries have to make. If one is to use Blue Grouse as a model, however, they ultimately lead to success. The winery's output may be small, its selections heavy on aromatic whites, but the wines are exceptional across the board, the whites all perfect accompaniments to local shellfish and produce, the reds well suited to fresh-caught salmon or Cowichan Valley-raised duck.

Though Kiltz is reluctant to ascribe any characteristics of *terroir* to his particular property, he does believe Vancouver Island has something special. "Certainly

the wines we make on the island are different than, say, the same varieties from the Okanagan. Our wines usually have lots of fruit, maybe a shorter finish, maybe a bit more acidity. I don't know if it's as much the soil, or more the climate."

Whatever it is, Kiltz is figuring it out, along with the rest of his fellow island winemakers.

The vineyards at Blue Grouse were carved out of the dense, Douglas fir-clad forests of the Cowichan Valley. Keeping the critters, like black bears and deer, from eating the grapes is nearly a full-time endeavour.

The team at Cherry Point Estate Wines gathered beside their outdoor patio and bistro for a brief respite from the hectic pace of the fall grape harvest and crush. Left and middle: owners Maria and Xavier Bonilla. Right: new winemaker Dean Canadzich

CHERRY POINT
ESTATE WINES

Established in 1990, and producing wine since 1994, Cherry Point has a storied history which added a new chapter in late 2009, when the Khowtzun Development Corporation (KDC), the economic-development arm of the Cowichan First Nation in Duncan, sold the winery to Xavier and Maria Bonilla. The KDC had purchased the winery in 2004 from founders Wayne and Helena Ulrich, but decided to put it up for sale after just five years (and many improvements to the facility).

Though the Bonillas, who previously owned a restaurant in West Vancouver, had actually wanted to buy Cherry Point from the Ulrichs in 2004, they weren't able to complete the deal at the time. Nonetheless, they maintained a keen interest in it and when the KDC decided to sell in 2009, they were finally able to purchase the business and property they had longed to own. "I had some very specific criteria for the kind of farm that I wanted," explains Xavier Bonilla, a native of Ecuador, who, along with Maria, has been a Canadian citizen for eight years. "Cherry Point has certain characteristics that attracted us."

Part of that attraction for the Bonillas is reflected in the slight name change they made to the business shortly after taking possession. What was previously Cherry Point Vineyards is now Cherry Point Estate Wines. The couple are firm believers in the quality of the 20-acre vineyard's *terroir* and they want their wines to reflect that. "The grape does not make the wine, it's the earth," says Bonilla. "You plant what is best for the land. And when you drink our wines, you feel the aromas of this earth, this land. Even within the property there are differences. It's amazing."

With the Bonillas taking over from the Cowichan First Nation, Cherry Point has returned to being a family-run endeavour, something the couple felt strongly about. "When it was owned by the [KDC], it was more of a corporate approach," says Bonilla. "It had set hours of operation; it opened in the morning and closed in the evening. Now it's a family-owned operation and we're here 24 hours a day, my wife and I. Our two children are at the University of British Columbia, but they also come to help on the bottling line and to help in many aspects of the farm now."

One thing that initially remained the same at Cherry Point was winemaker Simon Spencer's role. Because he had been at the winery since 2003 and he knew the vineyard and its varieties—Ortega, Pinot Gris, Gewurztraminer, Siegerrebe, Pinot Noir, Agria—he was retained by the Bonillas to make their transition a

Best Vintages: 2003–2006, 2009

Open to the Public: Yes
(check website for hours)

840 Cherry Point Road
Cobble Hill
T: 250-743-1272
E: cherrypointvineyards.com/contact.cfm
W: cherrypointestatewines.com

smooth one. Though he had worked in France's warm, Mediterranean Languedoc region prior to coming to Cherry Point, he appreciates what the cooler island climate offers. "We don't have as many heat units as other areas," Spencer explains, "so the wines we can make here are quite a bit more fruit forward and crisp, with decent acidity. I haven't been afraid of bottling wines with higher than average acids. People are liking these types of wine with food."

Which will, no doubt, please diners at the winery's bistro, another part of Cherry Point that the Bonillas are putting their own touch on. "It's going to have some very interesting dishes," says Bonilla, "with a touch of Spain—tapas, and things like that—to be paired with our wines."

And, of course, one of Cherry Point's most iconic offerings—its blackberry, dessert-style wine—remains an important part of their business (it accounts for more than half of their annual production, which varies between 4,000 and 10,000 cases), and a great way to keep the community involved in the winery. "Children from all over the valley bring the wild blackberries, which we buy from them," says Bonilla. "This [wine] has been very well accepted by the community and people ask for it from all over. Of course, we will continue with that."

The Bonillas have most certainly put their own imprint on Cherry Point, but in many ways they have simply returned it to the Ulrichs' original ideals—a belief

in the quality of the land and the wonderful grapes that can be grown here. "We are committed to producing all of our wines here," Bonilla says. And they showed that commitment in early 2010 by pulling out vines that weren't suitable and doing well, and replanting with red Blattner varieties like Petit Milo and Cabernet Libre, among others. "With the disease resistance of [these vines], they're quite appealing," says Spencer, who has since been replaced by Australian winemaker Dean Canadzich. Bonilla concurs, adding, "When looking for plants, you want a healthy plant, but you want a plant that is for *this* land."

An enormous, old, winemaking barrel greets visitors arriving at Cherry Point Estate Wines.

This summer day on Salt Spring Island was unusually misty and foggy as we toured Garry Oaks Winery with owner/winemaker Elaine Kozak. The winery cat is a constant companion.

GARRY OAKS
WINERY

In 1999 Elaine Kozak and Marcel Mercier identified the property on Salt Spring Island where they wanted to start their winery before they even knew if it was for sale. As it turned out, the octogenarian widow who owned the 100-year-old farm was intrigued by their proposed endeavour and agreed to sell on the condition that she be allowed to stay on the property for a period of time until she'd had a chance to arrange her own move.

The couple had been thorough in their research and were certain that this would be the place to start their new adventure. "The site is what we consider to be one of the best growing sites in the wine islands," says Mercier, who is in charge of the vineyard, while Kozak does the winemaking. "We're in the middle of the mountain and we overlook the Burgoyne Valley. It's a nice, sandy, gravelly slope that's perfectly south-facing to receive the sun. We get very good air and water drainage, too."

They planted their first vines in 2000 and now have a total of seven acres of Pinot Noir, Pinot Gris, Gewürztraminer, Chardonnay, and Zweigelt, an Austrian

red variety that is uncommon in North America. "[Zweigelt] is a medium-bodied, very dark red," explains Mercier. "It kind of falls between a Pinot Noir and Bordeaux-style. The flavours are black cherry fruit and lots of spice. It's a very spicy grape, with really nice tannins on it and nice acidity."

Though the winery's other varietals are better known and somewhat standard for the area, the couple didn't exactly take the tried-and-tested route in every regard, choosing, for instance, an Alsatian [French] clone of Gewürztraminer instead of a German one and grafting the vines on rootstock that no one in the area had used before. "All of those things—the varieties, the clones, the site—work really well together," says Mercier. "We get a lot of people asking us if we were to start again would we choose something different, and we wouldn't."

Though they currently offer one non-estate wine, a Bordeaux-style blend called Fetish made from Okanagan grapes, it will finally be phased out with the release of the 2007 vintage in 2011. In fact, they haven't bought from the Okanagan since 2007. "We've decided to focus entirely on estate-grown grapes," confirms Mercier of their 1,500-case annual production. "The estate wines we have are all 100 percent grown here on our site."

The modest vineyard has been producing since 2002, Garry Oaks' first vintage, and with eight vintages under their belts now, Mercier and Kozak have definitely

Best Vintages: 2004–2006, 2009

Open to the Public: Yes
(check website for hours)

1880 Fulford-Ganges Road
Salt Spring Island
T: 250-653-4687
E: info@garryoakswine.com
W: garryoakswine.com

detected some consistency in the flavours produced by the *terroir*, no matter what the weather is like in a given season. "In the Pinot Gris, there's a nice mineral aspect to it," explains Mercier, "particularly in the finish. You're also going to get flavours of pear and passion fruit, or pear and peach with a nice citrusy finish on it. With the Pinot Noir there's always that fresh raspberry and usually cherry that you get on it."

Through the relatively short history of island winemaking there has been a constant cry from doubters that, by the North American standard of what a wine region should be like, this area is simply not suitable for grape growing. Mercier, however, has a much more optimistic take. "A lot of people think that grapes require a really hot climate, but you select grapes for the climate that you have, and the French have always said that you get the best expression of the fruit at the northern edge of [a grape's] climate zone. Of course, we're at the northern edge for the varieties that we grow here, these cool-climate grapes."

And perhaps Garry Oaks' success in growing excellent wine grapes comes down to the fact that they *did* find the best spot for a vineyard on Salt Spring Island, because in both tough years and good ones they have fared well. "Every year we've had really good grapes, even in 2007 and 2008, which were very difficult years in both British Columbia and Washington," says Mercier. "2007 was a

cool year; there wasn't much sun. And in 2008 we had a really late spring—almost four weeks late. We came through really well in terms of both the quality of the fruit and the yield. I think that's a real testimonial to the site and what we're trying to do here."

After a busy day at Garry Oaks Winery on Salt Spring, we stop to look out over the south-facing slope of the Burgoyne Valley toward the now-quiet tasting room.

Glenterra Vineyards owners John Kelly and Ruth Luxton in their tasting room, an inviting and casual blend of old meets modern where restored antique windows are brightened with a burst of colour from a vase of fresh-picked local flowers.

GLENTERRA
VINEYARDS

One need only look at the grape varieties used in Glenterra's two blends—Vivace (white) and Brio (red)—to get a glimpse of the early days of Vancouver Island viticulture. Ehrenfelser, Wurzer, Huxelrebe, Reichensteiner, Dornfelder, Dunkelfelder, Frühburgunder, Haroldrebe, and Helfensteiner are varietal names that are certainly not familiar to most wine enthusiasts, but these are just some of the cool-climate varietals that were experimented with in the 1980s when people were trying to determine the viability of making wine on Vancouver Island.

So, why are Glenterra owners John Kelly and Ruth Luxton still making wine from these obscurities? The simple answer is that their property previously belonged to John Harper, the pioneering island viticulturist who was key in establishing what grapes would do well here, and when they bought it in the late 1990s it still had a one-acre experimental vineyard packed with 40 different varieties. A good number of those—enhanced by more familiar grapes like Pinot Gris, Pinot Blanc, Ortega, Pinot Noir, and others—end up in Glenterra's popular

blends every year. In their own way, they're keeping a part of Vancouver Island's winemaking roots alive.

Though Vancouver Island wasn't the first place the couple considered for starting their own winery after Kelly completed two years of course work in viniculture and viticulture at Okanagan University College in Penticton, it was ultimately the place that felt like the best fit. The Okanagan may have been the obvious place to settle at the time, but the wetter side of the province beckoned. "Financially it may have been a better move, because the industry is so much more established [in the Okanagan]," says Kelly, "but we were from the coast and the coast was sort of where we wanted to be. The only other area where there was a viable wine region at that particular time—the late '90s—was here in the Cowichan Valley."

Kelly and Luxton joined the ranks of their well-established Cowichan Valley neighbours—Cherry Point, Blue Grouse, Alderlea, Vigneti Zanatta and Venturi-Schulze—when they opened Glenterra for business in 2000. The one-acre experimental vineyard was obviously kept intact, but it has been augmented over the years by extensive plantings of Pinot Gris, Pinot Noir, and Gewürztraminer—Glenterra's regular offerings.

Two additional acres of newer Pinot Noir clones were planted in 2010, upping the vineyard to eight acres. "We're hoping to build up the different clones of the

Best Vintages: 2004, 2006, 2009

Open to the Public: Yes
(check website for hours)

3897 Cobble Hill Road
Cobble Hill
T: 250-743-2330
E: wine@glenterravineyards.com
W: glenterravineyards.com

Pinot Noir to get a little more complexity in the long term," says Kelly of the new vines.

Glenterra only produces 750 cases per year and still augments its offerings with some Okanagan grapes, so the Thistles Café—complete with a lovely vineyard-side patio—has become an integral part of the business as well. Luxton runs that side of things and opts to buy local and organic as much as possible, a philosophy that is also at play in the vineyard. Though Glenterra isn't certified organic, they have been "clean" for almost a decade and have farmed completely organically, which is not, as we know, the path of least resistance. "We do put a lot of extra labour into our vineyard," says Kelly. "We thin out all the excess lateral growth, so there's airflow through the vineyard, so we don't have to use systemic fungicide."

They also don't irrigate their vines, which Kelly believes adds to the character of the wines he makes. "We get smaller berry weights, but we get more intense flavours from our berries. Sometimes the sugar levels are a little lower, but that's okay. We can work with that if the flavour profile's there in the grapes. We want as much flavour as possible in the fruit."

And all this—the dry, organic farming—really lets the character of the land shine through. Kelly is a firm believer that this is a special wine-growing region,

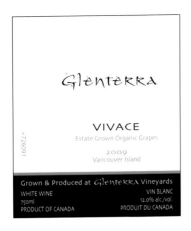

Glenterra

VIVACE

Estate Grown Organic Grapes

2009
Vancouver Island

Grown & Produced at Glenterra Vineyards
WHITE WINE   VIN BLANC
750ml   12.0% alc./vol.
PRODUCT OF CANADA   PRODUIT DU CANADA

with unique *terroir*, and he tastes it in his own wines. "All of the whites, every year, have a lovely citrusy, grapefruity, and subtle lemon note, and definitely a nice sort of minerally streak through them," he says. "Island Pinot [Noir], in general, always has this wonderful little black pepper note that comes out in just about everybody's."

Kelly and Luxton are happy to have settled on Vancouver Island to start their winery rather than in the Okanagan. It may be more challenging in many regards—not the least of which is the need to familiarize the public with some of the varieties that grow best on the island (and are found in abundance in Glenterra's blends)—but great wine is being made here and ultimately, that's what will make the region's reputation. "Some people say that Vancouver Island is too marginal [as a grape-growing region]," Kelly says, "but I say, 'try our wines.'"

Thistles Café, at Glenterra Vineyards, offering a menu featuring fresh, local, and seasonal foods, is a good place to pause and refuel while exploring the Vancouver Island wine trail.

Owners/winemakers Keith Watt and Barb Reid are engaging hosts, ardent foodies and avid art collectors. Morning Bay Vineyard and Estate is their oceanfront, gravity-fed winery on Pender Island, one of more-than-a-dozen southern Gulf Islands between Vancouver Island and BC's mainland. Here, they keep it light and bright with glasses of their favourite rosé—Morning Bay Estate Chiaretto, of course.

MORNING BAY
VINEYARD & ESTATE
WINERY

For Morning Bay Vineyard & Estate Winery owners Keith Watt and Barbara Reid, the inspiration to start a winery on their 25-acre oceanfront property on Pender Island came from across the water. Watt was looking out his window toward Saturna Island one sunny day in the late 1990s when he noticed something unusual. "I could see funny stripes," he recounts with amusement, "and the sun was glinting off something that looked like steel wire. So I hopped in my boat and went across to see what was going on, and saw, in fact, that [it was] a vineyard, Saturna Island Family Estate Vineyard, which is directly across the water from us."

Watt and Reid had owned their Pender Island property since 1992 and were wondering what they could do with it in terms of farming that would be profitable. Wine, they surmised, could potentially do that, as well as satisfy some other requirements. "I was hoping to do something that would keep me on the island," says Watt. "Something that we could grow and enjoy ourselves and something that we could share with people. And when I saw that somebody else had planted grapes, I began to investigate grapes as a crop on our property. It turned out that

our farm is steep, south-facing, and rocky—perfect for growing grapes. That is when I began to concoct a plan."

That plan was nothing short of ambitious and was set into motion in 2002. Ten acres were cleared and terraced, miles of deer fence were erected, a million-gallon pond was dug and 5,000 vines were planted. That was just Year One. In 2003 they planned and designed the gravity-fed winery, and from 2004 to 2005 the gorgeous, innovative structure was built. "[It features a] concrete cube dug into the north side of a hill," says Watt, "which is a perfect ground-temperature-controlled wine storage area. The second floor—a kind of barn-like structure where we keep our stainless steel tanks—is made from trees we cut down to build the vineyard."

Reid and Watt were still, in fact, finishing their winery when they released their first vintage in 2005 using Okanagan grapes as well as their estate-grown grapes. Everything was finally finished in 2006 and that same year, they started selling their wine in restaurants and stores off the island. (Today it's sold as far afield as Saskatchewan.) Though the couple have continued to use Okanagan grapes to make their red offerings—Merlot, Syrah, Cabernet Sauvignon, and blends—they are also committed to making the most of their ten-acre estate vineyard planted with Pinot Noir, Pinot Gris, Gewürztraminer, Riesling, Schonburger, Ortega, and Marechal Foch. In fact, two of the winery's more iconic wines are the blends—

Best Vintages: 2006 and 2009 for estate-grown wines; 2006, 2008 for Okanagan-grown wines

Open to the Public: Yes (check website for hours)

6621 Harbour Hills Drive
Pender Island
T: 250-629-8351
E: morningbay.ca/winery-contact.php
W: morningbay.ca

Bianco (their white) and Chiaretto (their rosé)—Watt makes from estate grapes. "Blends are the way to go," says Watt, "particularly with island wines, because you get more characteristics of more different grapes and they make a more complex drink. We try to emphasize the aromatics in our winemaking and they're delightful, light 10.5 percent and 11 percent alcohol wines that are perfect for a summer afternoon on the patio. I think they're stylishly different from anything else that's on the market right now."

It's in these wines that Watt celebrates the special characteristics of island-grown grapes. "If you smell our wines, they're hugely aromatic," he says. "It's partly the varietals that do well here—like Gewürztraminer and Schonburger—but [our wines are] bigger on the nose than they are on the palate. They are higher-acid wines, food-friendly wines. They have fresh citrus flavors. These things all make [island-grown] wines unique." He sums up their reflection of the wine islands region: "I like to say about our wines that they're grown within sight of the ocean and they are tailor-made to go with the food in that ocean."

Though their estate-grown blends make up only about a quarter to a third of their annual 2,500-case production, Watt believes very strongly in them and their place in the modern North American wine world, which, he says, is still maturing. "In a more complex wine culture, there's a place for these wines, and I think what

we're seeing all up and down the west coast of North America is those wine cultures are getting more sophisticated. I really think that Morning Bay and the island wines are helping fill some niches in the local production, so that people looking for more varied wine experiences can find them."

If you're an early bird and get up at 6 AM, you could be rewarded with a magnificent sunrise from the top of a steep vineyard at Morning Bay. In the distance is Saturna Island.

Take the short 30 minute drive from Victoria to visit Muse Winery in the pretty Deep Cove area, located at the northern end of the Saanich Peninsula. Muse is a welcoming, three-acre boutique winery and gift store owned and operated by Jane and Peter Ellmann.

MUSE
WINERY

It's one thing to have the resources and wherewithal to purchase a winery, but truly making it your own—a reflection of who you are and what you believe in—is an altogether different challenge. When Peter and Jane Ellmann bought Chalet Estate Winery on the Saanich Peninsula in 2008, they knew they were getting an established business—a winery, bistro, tasting room, vineyard—that the previous owners, Michael Betts and Linda Plimley, had spent ten years nurturing, but they had no idea the connection they would feel to it. "Just coming down Tatlow Road with the vineyard in front of us and the cove, we knew that this was the place," says Peter of their search for a BC winery to buy.

And so Muse Winery was born. It's still located on Chalet Road, not far from the Swartz Bay ferry terminal and a stone's throw from Deep Cove, but most traces of its previous identity have been replaced by the images and words—and, more importantly, the wines—that the Ellmanns have created to represent their winery. Though there have been many changes—the labels are bright and playful now, the vines are even being trained differently in the vineyard, production has been

increased—Betts and Plimley's commitment to estate- and island-grown wines is being carried on by the new owners, even though they're still getting familiar with the region's unique *terroir*. "We're excited to learn about the island varietals," says Jane, "and we're committed to growing as much as we can of the varietals that do well here."

Their own vineyard is just three acres of (predominantly) Pinot Gris, Ortega, and Marechal Foch, lovingly protected from cool maritime breezes by tall stands of Douglas firs, but they source grapes from numerous other growers both on and off the island. Though the Ellmanns nearly purchased a winery in the Okanagan's Golden Mile area before finding Chalet Estate, they believe that they are able to get, in their words, the best of both worlds here on Vancouver Island. "What clinched the deal," Jane explains, "was that we could continue buying grapes from [previous owner] Michael's contacts in the Okanagan. So, we could still bring in some of the red wine grapes that we absolutely wanted to have, but couldn't grow here on the island."

The Ellmanns also kept Michael Betts on as a consulting winemaker to help bring them up to speed on the island varietals, something that Peter professes was initially all new territory for him. "I didn't know what Ortega was," he admits. "I thought it was a hot sauce. [Laughs] All those Germanic varietals—Siegerrebe,

Best Vintages: 2008 for Okanagan-grown reds; 2009 (best vintage since 2004) for island-grown reds and whites

Open to the Public: Yes
(check website for hours)

11195 Chalet Road
North Saanich
T: 250-656-2552
E: info@musewinery.ca
W: musewinery.ca

Ortega, and on and on—along with Marechal Foch, I had never done anything with those grapes." His experience, from working for more than two decades in the California wine industry, was mostly with big red varietals. "That's what I know, so that's why, working with Michael as a team, we're really having a lot of fun."

Making big reds from Okanagan grapes has also allowed the Ellmanns to dramatically boost their annual production. Chalet Estate was producing 1,800 cases annually, but Muse has bumped this number to 3,800 in 2008 and to approximately 4,200 in 2009. Not surprisingly, with the dramatic increase, they discovered they needed more space. In early 2010, they began construction on a new winemaking facility on the property.

But the increase in production isn't solely based on the selection of the big Okanagan-grown reds they're making—from Bordeaux-style blends to luscious Syrahs. Though their own estate vineyard is small, they have been actively sourcing grapes from six or seven different island growers, including the Deep Cove Chalet restaurant's small vineyard, right across the road. The Ellmanns may not grow all of the grapes used in their wines but they are big proponents of their local *terroir*—"We want our [island] suppliers close to us," Peter says—and they believe there is a specialness to the Saanich Peninsula. "There's a lot of clay here, and the Pinot Gris especially picks up more of the elements of the soil and its surrounding

flavours because it's truly sitting in a clay base. It picks up more from soil, which gives it an earthy flavour."

But like every other island winery, they've discovered that sense of place, that "island flavour," is sometimes a challenge for visitors to understand. "A lot of out-of-town visitors—especially people from Alberta—will come in to the tasting room and say, 'I'm only interested in tasting reds,'" says Jane. "'But, hey, you're visiting the island, you need to play my game. And if you're not happy with [the island wine], here's the dump bucket, but let's go through all the wines and give them a taste. Give them a chance.' Sure enough, they'll walk out the door with a bottle of Ortega and Pinot Gris, and they're huge new fans."

Surrounded by lush gardens and wine grapes seeming to slumber in the warm noonday sun, visitors can enjoy lunch on the outdoor patio.

Rocky Creek Winery is located just outside the small village of Cowichan Bay, which is one of the first communities in North America to become a Cittaslow (or Slow City) community. Owners/ winemakers Mark and Linda Holford are also believers in encouraging sustainability and ecotourism at their award-winning winery.

ROCKY CREEK
WINERY

Though starting a winery on Vancouver Island in 2004 was still a risky proposition—as with any business—the latest wave of island wineries that came on stream in the new millennium has enjoyed certain advantages that its forebears did not. One such benefit is having access to island-grown grapes from established vines long before your own vineyard is fully established.

Husband-and-wife team Mark and Linda Holford hit the ground running when they started Rocky Creek Winery out of their house in a Ladysmith subdivision. Since they weren't a "land-based" winery—that is to say, a winery on a plot of land where grapes are being grown for the wine—the licensing they received from the BC government allowed them to purchase grapes from anywhere in the world—Chile, USA, France—and make, like Mission Hill's sub-brands, "cellared in Canada" wines.

That, however, wasn't what the Holfords had in mind. "Our goal from the get-go was to do it with a 100 percent island-grown grapes," says Linda, "and it always has been." So, they leased a three-acre vineyard in Chemainus

planted with Ortega, Pinot Gris, Pinot Noir, Siegerrebe, Bacchus, Agria, and Gewürztraminer, and had their first crush in 2005. Though they describe the process as "doing it kind of backwards," the advantage was that they didn't need a huge initial investment to get the winery going, and they could basically start making and selling wine from the grapes on the leased vineyard right away. This then brought them the capital to buy the land in Cowichan Bay where the winery is currently located, and plant five and a half more acres—three of both red and white Blattner hybrids and two of thornless, cultivated blackberries for their popular blackberry dessert wine.

Rocky Creek's initial lineup of wines—Pinot Noir, Pinot Gris, Ortega, and the blackberry dessert wine—were in line with what other wineries on the island were offering, but the Holfords have augmented that with other wines, as the individual conditions of each vintage dictate. In 2008, for instance, the cool, wet summer required that the small amount of Pinot Noir they could make would need to be vinified differently to help concentrate the flavours. A rosé called Robin's Rosé was made from some of the grapes, and it proved to be a hit with customers. That same year they made their first sparkling wine, Katherine's Sparkler, from Bacchus, Gewürztraminer, and a touch of Ortega.

"Even in the tough years [like 2008]," says Mark, "if you know what to do with

Best Vintages: 2005, 2009

Open to the Public: Yes
(check website for hours)

1854 Myhrest Road
Cowichan Bay
T: 250-748-5622
E: info@rockycreekwinery.ca
W: rockycreekwinery.ca

the grapes to get the best out of them, then you can make a real nice wine. As long as you use some of the better techniques, and don't just assume you're going to do the same thing year after year after year. You have to look at the crop that you're getting and the quality, and where it's at, and try to make some good choices about what you do."

As a result of this tough vintage, they discovered that there was a good market for both rosé and sparkling wines and they plan to continue making them in the future, a decision enabled by their recent acquisition of a third vineyard (about two acres of Pinot Noir), also in Cowichan Bay. This brings their vineyard total to about ten acres, a size that suits the couple just fine, especially once the Blattner varieties are producing. They will go from their 2009 production of about 1,500 cases per year to 3,000 in just a few short years.

Though Rocky Creek isn't currently a certified organic winery, part of the Holfords' interest in working with the Blattner vines is their natural disease resistance. "My goal is to have an organic vineyard and to operate organically and there are very few white wine grapes that are resistant to powdery mildew," Mark says. "The Blattner whites have been selected for their resistance to powdery mildew. So we'll have a really good opportunity to have an organic commercial vineyard here." Additionally, the Blattner reds (whose parentage is part Cabernet Sauvignon)

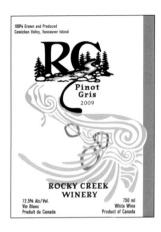

and which make up 75 percent of the vineyard at the winery, also offer Mark the opportunity to make a full-bodied red wine. "People want reds," says Linda, adding that with these experimental vines, they hope to deliver "that bold red that everybody wants."

Even though the Holfords' 2004 entry into the Vancouver Island winemaking scene was made a little easier by the work done by the first generation of island grape growers, they still face many of the same challenges that have existed here for more than 20 years.

"We're a bit like salmon swimming upstream, using Vancouver Island grapes," says Linda, "because people don't know about us yet. If we are true to our *terroir*, these wines won't taste like the Okanagan. We really do want you to taste what tastes different [about the grapes]."

A gorgeous fall day on the island. The last rays of a setting sun highlight the beauty of the area at Rocky Creek Winery.

The visitors are gone and the day is nearly done as Joanne and Dev McIntyre, owners of Salt Spring Vineyards, take pleasure in a last glass of wine before closing the tasting room doors and heading home.

SALT SPRING VINEYARDS

Joanne and Dev McIntyre have owned Salt Spring Vineyards for only two years, but they have more than two decades of experience growing cool-climate grapes in western BC. The couple, who purchased the winery from founders Jan and Bill Harkley in 2007, were perfectly suited to take on this endeavour, though they came to it with a slightly different—yet entirely relevant—geographic perspective. "Twenty-five years ago, long before there were really any grapes being grown on the coast, we started a little experimental vineyard on our acreage [in the Fraser Valley]," says Joanne about their early interest in wine and in grape growing. "There was a very keen group of people over there at the time called the Fraser Valley Grape Growers Association that got together to see if grapes could grow [in western BC]. We were growing grapes and making wine for 25 years over there, on just a hobby basis."

Though Salt Spring's climate is somewhat different from the Fraser Valley—Joanne describes it as a drier microclimate—the challenges of growing grapes are much the same throughout what she refers to as the "coastal" area of the Fraser

Valley, Gulf Islands, and Vancouver Island. Naturally, cool-climate varieties—from the Pinots (Noir and Gris) to the Riesling crosses (Ortega, Bacchus, Müller-Thurgau) and hybrids (Marechal Foch, Leon Millot)—are what do best here. The McIntyres, who already possess an understanding of this from the years they spent in their experimental vineyard, clearly embrace this.

The three-and-a-half-acre vineyard that came with the Salt Spring winery when they purchased it was, of course, planted with some of these varieties, but additional grapes are sourced across the road at their winemaker Paul Troop's ten-acre vineyard, as well as from select Salt Spring and Vancouver Island growers. They do make one wine (a Merlot) sourced from Okanagan grapes, but the McIntyres know that ultimately, the success of the island wine industry lies in making wines from local grapes that truly represent the area's strengths—in spite of the sometimes less-than-ideal growing conditions. "That's what this region has to do," Joanne states. "It has to, every year, consistently make good wines, even when the weather is not as cooperative."

It's basically like that old saying: "When life gives you lemons, make lemonade." In 2008, a "cold, rainy summer," the McIntyres' first vintage tested their fortitude right away and they were forced to make the best out of a tricky situation. "It was not a good year," says Joanne. "It's a testimony to Paul Troop's

Best Vintages: 2009 (outstanding sparkling wine, and Pinot Noir will be special. Current owners have only been there two years)

Open to the Public: Yes
(check website for hours)

151 Lee Road
Salt Spring Island
T: 250-653-9463
E: info@saltspringvineyards.com
W: saltspringvineyards.com

abilities as a winemaker that the wines were so good. When the fruit came in, I was frightened that we wouldn't have a vintage. But Paul made some excellent wines. Even in a not-so-good year, with a talented winemaker, you can produce good wine."

Though he didn't find their Pinot Noir grapes to be of sufficiently high quality to make a reserve vintage in 2008, Troop nonetheless produced a deliciously lip-smacking and fruity *blanc de noir* rosé that sold out very quickly and was a popular summer sipper. Things were easier in 2009. "2009 was the exact opposite [of 2008]," says Joanne. "It was a phenomenal year and it's a wonderful vintage."

Salt Spring Vineyards' offerings total about 2,200 cases a year and normally feature island *vinifera* essentials like Pinot Gris, Pinot Noir, and a sparkling wine made from Pinot Noir and Chardonnay, as well as an apple-based dessert wine and a blackberry port-style wine. Their Aromata is a blend of locally sourced cool-climate aromatic white varieties, while the Millotage is a blend of two hybrids—Marechal Foch and Leon Millot—which makes a nice table red, perfect for serving with hearty, tomato-based pasta dishes. Like Alderlea and Averill Creek on Vancouver Island, they are also utilizing some of the Blattner hybrid varieties and have already released a Cabernet Libre, in hopes that these vines will be able to produce big, mouth-filling reds in our cooler growing climate.

Perhaps one day these locally grown reds may replace the Okanagan-sourced Merlot in Salt Spring Vineyards' lineup. One thing is certain: the McIntyres, who "retired" from previous careers on the mainland to own the winery, don't want to grow much beyond what they're producing right now. "We may take it to 2,500 cases because of our Champagne-style wine," says Joanne, "but we want to keep it small and good. Our aim really is to make excellent wines, not volume wines. We're not in this to make a big commercial winery. This is our passion, really, and our size is good."

Overlooking the goose pond and
picnic area at Salt Spring Vineyards.

Danny Hattingh, Saturna Island Family Estate Winery winemaker, came here from South Africa to make wine in British Columbia. We hiked up a trail through the wildflowers to reach what is known as the Upper Vineyard. Watch out for the goats.

SATURNA ISLAND FAMILY ESTATE WINERY

Own a little piece of waterfront paradise on one of the Gulf Islands and aren't sure what to do with it? Well, Saturna Island Family Estate Winery proprietors Larry and Robyn Page—who bought the 80-acre, south-facing parcel in 1994 as a place to eventually retire—accidentally fell into the winemaking business when faced with that "conundrum".

"It was unheard-of to find a piece of property like that that was agriculturally zoned," explains hospitality manager Michael Vautour, who has been with the winery since its doors opened to the public in July of 1999. "The [Pages] did a subdivision of 20 acres along the waterfront and then were left with 60 acres of agriculturally zoned land, which was formerly pasture land for a sheep farm. They were toying with a couple of ideas when, by coincidence, an old friend of theirs returned from a two-year winemaking study in France and talked them into taking a swing at growing grapes."

The next four years were spent planting 48 acres of vines—Gewürztraminer, Pinot Gris, Pinot Noir, Merlot, Chardonnay, Pinot Meunier, and an experimental

field with two rows each of 14 other varieties—and building the tasting room, wine shop, bistro, and (temporary) winery. Though they made wines from Okanagan grapes for their first four vintages, until their own vines properly matured, the intent was always to focus on estate-grown wines.

A watermark year for Saturna Island Family Estate Winery was 2002. That's when construction of the permanent winery was completed and then-winemaker David Heard was able to make the first vintage of estate wines. "With a couple of exceptions, we have been producing all estate-grown wines since then," says Vautour. "On two occasions we have gone back to the Okanagan just to bump up the volume. But we've kept the [grapes] separate and done two different lines of wines, with two different labels, so that it's very clear what is estate grown and what isn't, and never did we mix them."

David Heard left the winery in 2008 and was replaced by Danny Hattingh, a young winemaker from South Africa, who brought along his partner, Megan De Villiers, to work as the viticulturist and field manager of the gorgeous, nearly waterfront vineyard. Though the bulk of the vines in that vineyard are Pinot Gris and Pinot Noir—the two wines for which Saturna Island Winery is best known—there's enough Gewürztraminer and Chardonnay for small varietal offerings, too. Hattingh also intends to start taking advantage of the fact that all three varietals

Best Vintages: 2006, 2007, 2009

Open to the Public: Yes
(check website for hours)

8 Quarry Road
Saturna Island
T: 250-539-5139 or 250-539-3521
TF: 1-877-918-3388
E: wine@saturnavineyards.com
W: saturnavineyards.com

used in traditional Champagne—Pinot Noir, Chardonnay, and Pinot Meunier—are being grown in the vineyard, and he has made a sparkling wine from the exceptional 2009 harvest, something the winery hasn't done since its very first vintage (using Okanagan grapes).

Though the quality of a winery should ultimately be judged by the wines it produces, it's hard for visitors here not to get swept up in the incredible beauty of the Saturna Island winery experience. Access is either by boat or car, and no matter how you arrive you're greeted by a scene almost too perfect to be real: rows of well-tended vines striping the gently sloped hills, with Mount Warburton Pike towering over them like a sentinel. And perched above the vineyard, overlooking the water, is the winery's bistro, complete with a lovely patio.

Gorgeous scenery aside, the setting also offers a very simple lesson in wine and food pairing. "All of our wines are on the lighter side and they're all wines that can be paired very nicely with seafood," notes Vautour, "so it's nice to be on a Gulf Island surrounded by water. When our bistro is open in the summertime, there's usually a bottle of Pinot Gris on almost every table."

The estate-grown Pinot Gris and Pinot Noir are two of the finer examples of what makes island-grown wine so special. They faithfully represent all the characteristics imbued by the long growing season and mild climate. They are fresh

and vibrant, and a great match for most locally grown and harvested foods—from Dungeness crab to Cowichan Valley duck. "The Pinot Noir is quite unique," says Vautour. "It's visually very light—people are sometimes taken aback by it until they have a taste and realize how pleasant it is. The Pinot Gris seems to be the star of the show. It has a lot of citrus notes and tropical fruit flavour to it. It's very well-rounded and well-balanced."

All characteristics that would no doubt be enhanced by the unbelievable setting should you find yourself enjoying these wines on the winery's patio on a slightly breezy but cloudless August afternoon.

The tasting room and restaurant at Saturna Island Family Estate Winery.

THE WINERY

Starling Lane Winery is located on the site of the old Heritage Farm—a local landmark—on Old West Saanich Road near Victoria. Winemaker John Wrinch, outside the winery and tasting room. You can just catch a glimpse of oak barrels through the doors.

STARLING LANE WINERY

Starling Lane Winery sits on a picturesque, rolling piece of land on the winding Old West Saanich Road. The winery and tasting room are located in a funky, converted barn that's perched near the modest, three-acre vineyard. Though this lovely property—owned by Jacqueline and John Wrinch—is the public face of Starling Lane, it's really just one part of the picture. Unlike most island wineries, which are generally family endeavours or run by husband-and-wife teams, this is a partnership between three such teams—all with their own Saanich Peninsula vineyards.

The Wrinches, Sue and Ken Houston, and Sherry and Jerry Mussio all began growing wine grapes on their own farms in the early 1990s and met while attending Vancouver Island Grape Growers Association meetings. "We were all growing our vineyards and sharing information as to what works and what doesn't," says Jerry Mussio. "Around 2000 or 2001, we all had ambitions of starting a winery, but each of our vineyards was two to three acres, which really isn't practical. Collectively, it sort of made sense. It's also quite expensive to [start a winery] on your own. So we thought it would make sense to collaborate."

Though all three grow grapes that go into the Starling Lane assortment—Pinot Noir, Marechal Foch, Ortega, Pinot Gris, rosé, sparkling wine, and a blackberry port-style wine—none of the couples are totally saddled with the numerous other tasks involved in running a winery. They've found an equitable way to divide up the labour that plays to each of their strengths.

"John, who lives here, has taken the lead on the winemaking," explains Mussio. "His wife, Jacqueline, looks after the tasting room and she hosts a lot of weddings here on the property as well, so she manages the coordinating between the weddings and the winery. Ken is the cellarmaster and looks after the winery itself. He looks after the barrels, all the equipment, and all that stuff. His wife, Sue, is our bookkeeper and looks after all of our accounts. Sherry, my wife, does all the artwork and the website and all that stuff. I do the marketing and sales."

Not surprisingly, all three couples are staunch supporters of and advocates for island-grown wines. "We always felt that, as far as we're concerned, our total commitment was going to be on island wines, where the objective would be to select grape varieties that grew well on the island." To that end, they have partnered with a fourth vineyard in the Cowichan Valley owned by Bente and Marcel Fleurie. The Fleuries aren't actively involved in Starling Lane, but their entire grape production is used by the winery.

Best Vintages: 2005, 2009 (a fantastic year)

Open to the Public: Yes
(check website for hours)

5271 Old West Saanich Road
Saanich
T: 250-881-7422
E: info@starlinglanewinery.com
W: starlinglanewinery.com

Theirs are the only grapes that the three couples aren't actively involved in growing, however, something that they feel is key to the quality of wine they can consistently produce. To that end, it's necessary that they regularly communicate to each other what's going on in their individual vineyards. "It's very important," Mussio says of the need to share information. "We're always talking about different pruning techniques or what seems to be working, or not, and how we select our fruit. It's part of the winemaking."

Since their first vintage in 2004, Starling Lane has produced an average of 1,000 cases per year, which always sell out. It's a modest amount of wine, but it's a good fit for the three couples who do it all themselves. "If we produce more," says Mussio, "we'd have to expand our vineyards, and currently we look after our own vineyards. We'd [also] have to hire people and then it becomes a different ball game."

In many ways, they represent the charm of island viticulture. Most wineries are small, their vineyards modest, and tasting rooms are staffed by one of the owners or their family. It's likely that, though it will no doubt grow, Vancouver Island and Gulf Island wine production probably will never be as big as its wine-growing "neighbours" to the east in the Okanagan. And that suits the folks at Starling Lane just fine. They want this area's wineries to truly reflect the climate, the land,

the people. "When you go to a particular part of the globe that's a wine-growing region," says Mussio, "you want to taste the wines that are produced in that region. You enjoy them for their particular character in that region.

"We're not trying to compete with the Okanagan, in terms of [trying to make] their wines. We're selecting grape varieties that do well on Vancouver Island and nurturing those grapes and building a market around that."

John Wrinch takes a walk through the vineyard at picturesque Starling Lane Winery.

Venturi-Schulze Vineyards' winemakers/owners Giordano Venturi and Marilyn Venturi (née Schulze) take immense pride in their wines and their vineyards. They are known for making wonderful, traditional-style Aceto Balsamico (balsamic vinegar) and for keeping some of the most immaculately tended vineyards in the region.

VENTURI-SCHULZE
VINEYARDS

Calling the Venturi-Schulze family Vancouver Island winemaking pioneers perhaps gives the impression that they are of an older generation, and that their ideas and beliefs are staid. Nothing could be further from the truth. First licensed in 1993, the Cowichan Valley winery, run by husband-and-wife team Giordano and Marilyn Venturi and daughter Michelle Schulze, made a name for itself by, as Marilyn explains, "being true to ourselves and giving people what we say we're going to give them."

The Venturi-Schulze vision started with the original 15-acre farm, purchased in 1987, where their first four acres of vines—all *vinifera* grapes—were planted. Like others at the time, they were navigating uncharted territory, and figuring out what grapes would ripen properly, given the island climate and soil, which required some experimentation. However, like their fellow pioneers at Vigneti Zanatta and Blue Grouse, they quickly zeroed in on three Pinots (Noir, Gris, and Auxerrois). These have become island mainstays, along with some of the cold-climate, Riesling-related crosses like Siegerrebe, Ortega, Kerner, and Bacchus. What they then did with these grapes, however, was entirely unique.

Winemaker Giordano Venturi was born and raised in Modena, Italy, in an area where, according to Marilyn Venturi, "everyone made wine." Immigrating to Canada in 1967, he kept his interest in wine alive by planting backyard vineyards with cool-climate varietals. By the time he and Marilyn started Venturi-Schulze—the realization of a dream for both—he came to it with a degree of confidence and experience that perhaps some of his peers at the time lacked. And his approach to making wines—and other products such as their highly regarded balsamic vinegar and newest addition, verjus—has reflected that confidence.

As a result, Venturi-Schulze has not necessarily been known for one specific wine or varietal that they produce year in and year out. Certainly there are some that have been mainstays and are responsible for the winery's success and renown; one of those is the sparkling Brut Naturel, for instance, an Alsatian *crémant*-style sparkler made primarily from Pinot Gris and Pinot Auxerrois grapes and first bottled in 1991. Yet even these vary from vintage to vintage. "Our philosophy is basically that we're not trying to do the same things every year," confirms Marilyn. "We thoroughly embrace the fact that the seasons can be quite different and you can make wines that are reflecting that season and are really true to what the land and climate are offering. That's the beauty of being a small vineyard and making really small batches of wine."

Another benefit to keeping it small—they average about 2,000 cases per year

Best Vintages: 1992, 1994, 1996, 1998, 2000–2006, 2009

Open to the Public: Yes
(check website for hours)

4235 Vineyard Road
Cobble Hill
T: 250-743-5630
E: venturischulze.com/contact
W: venturischulze.com

of total production—is the ability to keep it all in the family. Daughter Michelle Schulze, the vineyard manager and assistant winemaker, has been an integral part of the operation since she graduated from high school in 1994. As the business has grown, she has taken on tasks previously handled solely by her parents. For Marilyn, who now finds herself occupied mostly in the winery lab and in dealing with the extensive government reporting necessary to run the business, her daughter's efforts have been invaluable to Venturi-Schulze's success. "She is an enormous part of the operation," says Marilyn. "She's amazing. She works extremely long hours. She's done every job here, from preparing the land to putting in posts, doing the wiring and planting vines."

Despite Venturi-Schulze's family operation and small size (though the four acres originally under vine have been expanded to 18), their product assortment, year in and year out, is one of the most diverse and interesting on the island. A toothsome mix of sparkling, still, and dessert wines, as well as the vinegar and verjus (pure, unfermented grape juice pressed from unripe fruit), many of these products are served at some of the finest restaurants in BC and beyond. "I'm very glad we have a variety of wines, because if you have all of your eggs in one basket, there may be years where you just don't get anything," says Marilyn. "It's been a good decision for us to maintain about eight good varieties."

They use those varieties somewhat differently from year to year. Their Pinot Noir and Zweigelt (another cool-climate red variety) from the challenging 2007 vintage, for instance, were used to make a dry *white* wine called The Bad Boys. Nevertheless, they believe quite firmly that there is a specialness about their *terroir*. "As far as I'm concerned, the wines from our property are absolutely distinct," says Marilyn. "There's definitely a certain aspect of minerality, which is difficult to put into words, that is quite distinct."

As is their entire approach to winemaking. And though it may seem unorthodox to some—they seal their sparklers with a cap, "all the better to preserve it"—Venturi-Schulze has a dedicated following that simply appreciates the quality inherent in whatever product the family puts its name on. "We want people to know that if they're going to drink our wine, it's going to be the absolute best that we can do. It doesn't mean that everyone's going to like all of our wines, but they're gonna know that the grapes are pure and unsprayed and absolutely perfect when they go in the picking bucket."

Following in the family footsteps: Venturi-Schulze Vineyards winemakers/owners Giordano and Marilyn Venturi are joined by daughter Michelle Schulze in the original Cobble Hill vineyard.

Winemaker Loretta Zanatta. Harvesting ripe, high-quality grapes is crucial to making fine wine at Vigneti Zanatta.

VIGNETI
ZANATTA

Call it faith or forward thinking, Dennis Zanatta had a hunch that Vancouver Island could produce some great wines. His 120-acre farm in the Glenora area of the Cowichan Valley, southwest of Duncan, was originally a dairy farm and he was actually in the stone and tile business. But the Italian-born Zanatta, one of 11 children from a farming family near Venice, planted some grape vines for his own use, purchasing them from the old federal research station in Saanich just to try things out here and there. One day in the 1980s, he was approached by a provincial government agent, John Vielvoye, and asked whether he'd be interested in growing additional wine grapes in an experimental vineyard on his land.

Zanatta agreed, providing Vielvoye and his crew with an acre on which they tried various cool-climate *vinifera* varieties like Schonburger, Kerner, Siegerrebe, Ortega, and Pinot Auxerrois, as well as hybrids like Cayuga, New York Muscat, Seyval Blanc, and Okanagan Riesling. When funding for that government program ran out, Zanatta continued to farm the grapes himself and simply allowed

the government to take what they needed for their winemaking research station in Summerland. He made wine with the rest, discovering on his own what varieties suited his land.

"Dad was really keen on the results of the Ortega especially, and the Cayuga," explains his daughter, Loretta Zanatta, who, along with her husband, Jim Moody, makes the wine for Vigneti Zanatta today. "So we decided to plant five acres of those varieties." Though the Zanatta family wasn't yet producing wine commercially, Dennis, who died in 2008, had definitely passed on his love of wine and grapes to his daughter, who first got a degree in plant science at the University of British Columbia and then studied winemaking—with an emphasis on sparkling wine—with a relative in northern Italy.

Her return to the family farm in 1990 happened to coincide with a change in provincial vineyard estate licensing, so that now only two acres of grapes were needed, rather than 25, to make and sell wine to the public. The family applied and produced their first vintage of Ortega in 1992. "When we opened, we were the only winery [in the area]," says Loretta, "so it was really complicated trying to get our wine into beer and wine stores. There was a lot of ground to break."

Nonetheless, Dennis Zanatta clearly saw the potential to grow good grapes on the land and encouraged his daughter to stick with it. "We started expanding

Best Vintages: 1998, 2000 (for reds),
2005 (Pinot Noir), 2006, 2007 (Ortega), 2009

Open to the Public: Yes
(check website for hours)

5039 Marshall Road
Duncan
T: 250-748-2338
E: zanatta@zanatta.ca
W: zanatta.ca

in 1992, before we knew how well it would do. Dad had a lot of faith in the industry. There were great changes coming. He was always a real forward thinker. He just started planting east. He started with the Ortega vineyard, which is our most western vineyard, and then he continued along the same slope and planted Pinot Auxerrois and Pinot Gris. He had the highland cleared—the higher hill with the nice gravelly soil—and he put in the Pinot Noir and Muscat. He just wanted those slopes planted. He said, 'Plant it now and it should be good, but if you want to change or the market changes, then pull it out. But at least you have your infrastructure and you're ready to go.'"

Today, Vigneti Zanatta produces about 3,000 cases a year. The bulk of that is dedicated to their unique and very popular Damasco white wine, a floral, fruity and slightly *frizzante* blend of some of the very varieties Dennis had the foresight to put in—Ortega, Pinot Auxerrois, Muscat, and Madeleine Sylvaner. But they also have several tasty sparkling offerings (including one made with the unique Cayuga grape), as well as other cool-climate varietals. The winery, a restaurant, Vinoteca, and a tasting room all occupy the Zanatta family's old farmhouse, and there are currently 30 acres under vine. Not surprisingly, all the grapes used for Zanatta wines are estate-grown. And Loretta, having tasted wines made here for more than 20 years, definitely believes there is a distinct Vancouver Island *terroir*,

due mostly to what some may feel is a negative: the weather. It's something that, in her opinion, actually encourages two classic Alsatian varietals, Pinot Noir and Pinot Gris, to do particularly well here.

"I can tell a Pinot Gris that's grown on Vancouver Island as opposed to one that's an Okanagan quite quickly," she says. "The Okanagan tends to be a fruitier wine and ours tends to be a bit more earthy. I find the Pinot Noirs on Vancouver Island are much fruitier and have much more spice to them than the Okanagans. I really believe it's because we have a long growing season. We may not start up great guns like the Okanagan does, where once things get warm, they get very warm and everything buds out. Here it's the really slow release of the bud, the slow flowering, slow everything. And it just carries on through October, and with that longer season, I think the flavours are developing much better in those sorts of varietals."

And thanks to her father's tremendous leap of faith in believing that Vancouver Island could produce fantastic wines, Loretta's been able to prove him right using, among others, Pinot Gris and Pinot Noir grown on the very vines he put in more than two decades ago.

A peek inside the Vigneti Zanatta wine production facility.

Early in the season at Averill Creek Vineyards in the Cowichan Valley. Note the stony ground around the vines that helps give the wines their unique terroir.

MORE WINERIES

Carbrea Vineyards & Winery
Proprietors: Stephen and Suzie Bishop
1885 Central Road, Hornby Island
Open to the Public: Yes (check website for hours)
Products/Wines: Pinot Noir, Pinot Gris, Gewürztraminer, Agria, blackberry dessert wine
T: 250-335-1240 | E: info@carbreavineyard.com | W: carbreavineyard.com
Comments: Carbrea makes "small lots of handcrafted wines"—with both estate-grown and Okanagan grapes—that aren't seen widely outside the Gulf Island/Vancouver Island area. All the more reason to hop on a ferry and visit the charming facility in person.

Church and State Wines
Proprietor: Kim Pullen
1445 Benvenuto Avenue, Brentwood Bay
Open to the Public: Yes (check website for hours)
Products/Wines: Pinot Gris, Chardonnay, Merlot, Syrah, Pinot Noir, Quintessential, Cabernet Sauvignon
T: 250-652-2671 | W: churchandstatewines.com
Comments: One of the larger wineries/tasting rooms on Vancouver Island, Church and State was originally called Victoria Estate Winery under previous ownership. Though the Saanich Peninsula facility (just up the road from Butchart Gardens) is surrounded by vineyards, most of the wines produced here are made with grapes grown in the Okanagan, where they have another winery in Oliver. You won't exactly get a true taste of island terroir here, but Church and State does big reds well, there are a couple of wines that are made from grapes grown on the island, and the patio restaurant overlooking the vineyard—open Wednesday to Sunday 11:30 AM to 3:30 PM— is a pleasant place to stop for lunch.

Deol Estate Winery
Proprietor: Gary Deol
6645 Somenos Road, Duncan
Open to the Public: Yes (check website for hours)
Products/Wines: Pinot Noir, Gamay Noir, Marechal Foch, Somenos Red, Pinot Gris, Gamay Rosé, Iced Chardonnay, Blanc De Noir
T: 250-746-3967 | E: info@deolestatewinery.com | W: deolestatewinery.com
Comments: Though this 18-acre vineyard was established a decade ago, the grapes grown here were originally sold by the Deol family to other local wineries. They released their first vintage in 2008 and are among a new generation of island wineries fully dedicated to using 100 percent estate-grown grapes.

Divino Estate Winery

Proprietor: Joe Busnardo

1500 Freeman Road, Cobble Hill

Open to the Public: Yes (check website for hours)

Products/Wines: Pinot Noir, Gamay Noir/Cabernet Sauvignon, Merlot/Cabernet Sauvignon, Chardonnay, Pinot Grigio, Piccolo Bianco

T: 250-743-2311 | E: info@divinowine.ca | W: divinowine.ca

Comments: Divino was originally Okanagan-based in the twilight of the modern BC wine industry (the early '80s), but the family relocated to Vancouver Island in the mid-'90s and currently has 40 acres under vine.

Dragonfly Hill Vineyard

Proprietor: Carol Wallace

6130 Old West Saanich Road, Saanich

Open to the Public: Yes (check website for hours)

Products/Wines: Ortega/Auxerrois, Chardonnay, Merlot/Cabernet Sauvignon, Bumbleberry dessert wine

T: 250-652-3782 | E: carol@dragonflyhillvineyard.com | W: dragonflyhillvineyard.com

Comments: Situated on what was once apple orchards and strawberry fields, this 18-year-old vineyard now grows a handful of cool-climate white varieties, such as the Pinot Auxerrois and Ortega used to make their popular aromatic blend. Their only other local wine is the Bumbleberry dessert wine made with island-grown berries. Both their Cab/Merlot and Chardonnay feature Okanagan grapes.

Godfrey-Brownell Vineyards

Proprietor: Dave Godfrey

4911 Marshall Road, Duncan

Open to the Public: Yes (check website for hours)

Products/Wines: Bacchus, Chardonnay, Pinot Gris, Pinot Noir, Gamay Noir, Marechal Foch

T: 250-715-0504 | E: gbvineyards@gmail.com | W: gbvineyards.com

Comments: This unusual winery tucked deep into the forest and farms of Glenora (just southwest of Duncan) sells most of its wine from its tasting room. The sunny outdoor patio is always buzzing with visitors enjoying small plates, featuring local ingredients, and glasses of wine in the summer. The 19-acre home vineyard was planted in the late '90s, while a second vineyard (ten acres) on Mount Prevost (northwest of Duncan) was planted in the mid-'00s. All wines are estate grown.

Mistaken Identity Vineyards

Proprietors: Ian and Wendy Baker, Dave and Lenora Baker, Cliff Broetz and Barb Steele

164 Norton Road, Salt Spring Island

Open to the Public: Yes (check website for hours)

Products/Wines: Pinot Rosé, Gewürztraminer, Pinot Gris, Abbondante Bianco (white estate blend), Pinot Noir, Merlot, Abbondante Rosso (red estate blend), Charmela (dessert wine)

T: 250-538-9463 | TF: 1-877-918-2783 | E: info@mistakenidentityvineyards.com

W: mistakenidentityvineyards.com

Comments: Their certified organic vineyard was planted in 2001, but the three couples involved in Mistaken Identity didn't purchase the property until 2007. They opened their doors in 2009 and produce primarily estate-grown wines, augmented with some certified organic fruit from the Okanagan.

SouthEnd Farm Vineyards

Proprietors: Ben McGuffie and Jill Ogasawara

319 Sutil Road, Quadra Island

Open to the Public: Yes (check website for hours)

Products/Wines: Ortega, Sutil (dessert Agria), Miwa (late-harvest Ortega), Jimmy K (sparkling Pinot Gris), Black Crow (Dornfelder, Agria, and Pinot Noir blend)

T: 250-285-2257 | E: info@southend.ca | W: southend.ca

Comments: A small Quadra Island endeavour run by a young couple "dedicated to making quality wine from 100 percent Quadra Island-grown grapes."

Twenty Two Oaks Winery

Proprietors: There are four families involved, including the MacLeods. Jeff MacLeod is the winemaker and vineyard manager.

1 – 6380 Lakes Road, Duncan

Open to the Public: Yes (check website for hours)

Products/Wines: Pinot Gris, Syrah, Syrah/Marechal Foch, Red Wine (Gamay, Merlot, Syrah)

T: 250-709-0787 | E: twentytwooakswinery@shaw.ca | W: 22oakswinery.ca

Comments: A newer winery located northeast of Duncan, whose vineyard and picnic area overlook Quamichan Lake. Currently most of their grapes are sourced from the Okanagan, but the six acres under vine at the winery do provide them with Pinot Gris, Marechal Foch, and Gamay Noir.

The Grapes
. . . and more

The arrival of the new leaf growth signals the beginning of the wine season and builds anticipation for the coming harvest.

TERROIR AND GRAPE VARIETALS

Treve Ring

Our islands—the wine islands—have a unique geography, climate, and *terroir* like nowhere else in the world. Within these Pacific isles, all terrains are spanned—from sandy beaches to rugged coastlines, marshy lowlands to rolling farmland, and lush, old-growth rainforests to snow-capped mountains. Vancouver Island is bisected by a mountain range, crossed by undulating rivers, and rimmed with countless bays of sheltered waters, strong tides, and dramatic coastlines. Between Vancouver Island and the mainland lie the Gulf Islands—numbering almost 100 in all.

Together, the islands boast the mildest climate in Canada. Our summers are reliably warm and sunny, with moderating westerly ocean breezes. Temperatures reach average highs in the mid-20s Celsius and cool considerably in the evenings, giving vines time to grow, and to rest. In winter months, the Vancouver Island region is the most temperate of all British Columbia, with temperatures just below zero degrees Celsius. Because of the abundant sunshine, relatively cool temperatures and dry summers, our grapes can attain a purity of varietal flavours seldom found elsewhere in the world.

The wine islands have their origin in volcanic rock, scoured by ice ages, revealing predominantly vine-loving clay, gravel, and sand soils. Our ground also benefits from very ancient terrane, a core formation created from undersea deposits near the Equator 380 million years ago. This oceanic terrane means our soils are limestone-rich, which explains the continuum of mineral notes inherent in our wines. Microclimates are different everywhere, with hills, rivers, and forests abutting each other, and pockets of sandy soil neighbouring rich clay loam. Though our coastal climate is mild in comparison to other major wine-growing regions in North America, it prevents us from reaching the high heat units required to ripen most varieties—especially reds. But great wines come from extreme places and we are certainly riding that edge. Proper site selection, varietal choice, and careful vinicultural techniques are needed to grow high-quality grapes and, in turn, create fine wines. So far, our very young industry on the island has shown promise in producing elegant and aromatic cool-climate grapes, similar to those in the noble areas of Europe. After all, at 49 degrees North, we are on the same latitude as parts of northern France and central Germany. The Burgundy region (Pinot Noir, Chardonnay, and Gamay grapes) and the Alsace region (Pinot Noir, Pinot Gris, Riesling, and Gewürztraminer grapes) are both located at 47 degrees North while the Champagne region (Chardonnay and Pinot Noir grapes) is at 49 degrees North.

A provincial government-funded trial, the Duncan Project, assessed about 100 different varieties between 1983 and 1990, and identified Pinot Gris, Auxerrois, and Ortega as promising varieties. Winemakers have made note of these pioneering farmers and their painstakingly planted trials. Crisp, fruity, and floral white grape varietals such as Ortega, Siegerrebe, and Pinot Gris dominate, while light to medium-bodied reds like Pinot Noir, Gamay, and Marechal Foch also turn up often. In the past few years, the increasing plantings of the Blattners have shown great promise, and will likely change the future of winemaking in this area.

But while there are the proven mainstays, there are also—like the winemakers themselves, experimental and sometimes temperamental—wild cards. As befits the independent and creative spirit of the islands, 40-plus varietals have been planted and commercially sold here. What defines the wines of the islands? In many ways, our wines are united more by their differences than by their similarities: style, technique, and purpose vary wildly. In general, there is a noticeable minerality to our wines, with crisp, clean fruit, bright acidity, and a refined character. These are not high-heat Okanagan fruit bombs but rather northern European-styled, lean, and food-friendly wines.

DOMINANT ISLAND VARIETIES

White Grapes

Auxerrois [OX-er-wha]

a.k.a.: Auxerrois Blanc, Pinot Auxerrois

This important white wine grape of Alsace is not to be confused with Auxerrois Gris (a.k.a. Pinot Gris). Nor is it to be confused with the red Auxerrois of France's Cahors region (a.k.a. Malbec or Cot). This Chardonnay sibling (both are crosses between Gouais Blanc and Pinot Noir) is often used with it in blends, along with the similar Pinot Blanc. While it is very susceptible to powdery mildew and labour intensive in the vineyard, the honeyed wine produced from the limestone-loving grapes is very attractive to winemakers.

Bacchus [BAK-us]

Aptly named for the Roman god of wine, this white wine grape was created by crossing Müller-Thurgau with Riesling and Sylvaner. While Bacchus may not be top of mind, or tip of tongue here, it is actually planted quite a bit, and is also found extensively in Germany and England. This early-budding, hardy, adaptable grape produces low-acid wines with floral muscat, citrus, and orange blossom flavours, and is often used in aromatic blends.

Chardonnay [shar-duh-NAY]

a.k.a.: Aubaine, Beaunois, Gamay Blanc, Melon Blanc, Chablis, White Burgundy, Mâconnais

Even if you know nothing at all about wines, you've no doubt heard of Chardonnay. You've probably even tasted it somewhere along your journey, as this is the most widely recognized white worldwide and therefore an obvious choice for the economies of the wine market. The Chardonnay grape itself is very neutral (making it excellent for sparkling wines), with many of the flavours

Ripe Pinot Gris grapes are ready to harvest

commonly associated with the grape coming from viticultural influences (*terroir*) and vinicultural techniques (oak). This hardy grape can be styled into crisp, apple- and mineral-flavoured wines or full, rich, buttery bombs. Because of our cooler climate, most winemakers tend to gravitate toward the leaner styles, though there are certainly highly oaked Chardonnays to be found here as well. Both oaked and unoaked styles are well suited to our local shellfish and poultry.

Gewürztraminer [geh-VERTZ-tram-in-er]

a.k.a.: Traminer

Gewürz translates as "spice" in German, which gives you some idea of the flavours of this aromatic white. Affectionately known as Gew ("goo"), it prefers cool climates, though it is particularly fussy about soils and very susceptible to disease, and it ripens erratically and late. However, the alluring, perfumed, floral nose and fuller-bodied enticing flavours of lychee make it hard for winemakers to resist. A natural high sugar content easily tilts this wine into the off-dry category. Gew can pair very well with local smoked salmon and semi-soft cheeses, as well as Asian flavours.

Ortega [or-TAY-guh]

This cross between Müller-Thurgau and Siegerrebe has become the premier white grape for the islands, and is said to be currently the most widely grown grape in the area. Ortega ripens early and easily, is not overly frost-sensitive, and achieves high must weights, which is why it is typically used for sweeter wines and blending in its native Germany. In Rheinhessen, where it is most common, the grape is used to enhance Riesling in poor vintages. Our Ortegas are peach-perfumed, light, crisp, limey whites, making them a terrific match for our local shellfish. Ortega was named in honour of the Spanish poet, philosopher, and wine-lover, José Ortega y Gasset.

Pinot Gris [PEE-noh GREE]

a.k.a.: Pinot Grigio, Auxerrois Gris, Rülander, Tokay d'Alsace, Grauer Burgunder, Fromentau, Malvoisie, Pinot Beurot, Petit Gris

There are two main styles of Pinot Gris on the islands: the first is a lean, unoaked, fruity, and crisp Italian Grigio-styled wine. The second is an oaked, spicy, richer wine in the Alsace style. The choice can depend on the warmth of the site and clone selection, but more typically it is vintner-driven. Whatever your preference, there is certainly a style for you here—the majority of wineries have Pinot Gris planted and release it as a single varietal. The Pinot Gris grape ripens earlier than Chardonnay and later than Ortega, creating nice insurance in the vineyard.

Schonburger [SHOWN-ber-ger]

a.k.a.: Schöenburger, Rosa Muskat, Geisenheim 15-114

Schonburger is a fairly recent cross of Pinot Noir with Chasselas and Muscat Hamburg. Though susceptible to powdery mildew, this cool-climate, reliable, early-ripening grape likes many soil types—all qualities appealing to vintners. But what seals the deal is the exotic spice, fig, citrus, and musk notes that make up this soft, fuller-bodied wine. Our islands' Schonburger is generally leaner and drier than Okanagan examples, which are fuller and sweeter. Outside of the Pacific Northwest, it is also seen in maritime-influenced regions of England and Germany.

Siegerrebe [zieg-ar-RAY-beh]

Siegerrebe is literally "victory vine" in German. A cross between Gewürztraminer and Madeleine Angevine, this very-early-ripening grape loves the cool coastal climates that help preserve its perfumed Muscat aroma and spicy pear taste. However, it can be susceptible to mildew, which is exacerbated by dampness, and wasps love the early, sweet, large grapes. Though it is low in acid, its high sugar potential and aromatic qualities lend themselves very well to blends, as well as to late-harvest wines.

Red Grapes

Marechal Foch [MAY-ray-shahl FOHSH]

Just as Ortega has made a name for itself as the islands' number one white, Marechal Foch is widely recognized as our leading red, whether we like it or not. Foch is a wine that people either love or love to hate—there's no middle ground. This hybrid was developed by Professor Kuhlmann, with the goal of creating a cold-tolerant, early-ripening, disease-resistant, full-bodied red. And reliability in the vineyard has proven a big asset—Foch ripens well even in cool vintages, producing a full, dark, and earthy red with softer tannins, making for early enjoyment (no cellaring required). Unfortunately, the small berry size makes this grape very appealing to birds. It is also seen in the northeastern United States, Ontario, and Quebec. In the 1980s, British Columbia had a massive pull-out of high-yielding North American vine species in order to change the industry's focus to quality wines. For the most part, Foch was among those vines that were yanked for more classic varieties like Cabernet Sauvignon, Merlot, and Pinot Noir. Luckily, a few growers saw Foch's potential, helping create an identity of wine that is unique to us. Older vines and low yields could make this a cult wine.

Pinot Noir [PEE-noh NWAHR]

a.k.a.: Blauer Spätburgunder, Blauer Klevner, Pinot Nero, Pineau

Another alias you could add to the above: The Heartbreak Grape. So named because of its temperamental nature and ability to move winemakers to tears. The beauty of Burgundy, and the grape responsible for some of the world's most highly regarded—and expensive—reds, it has proven to be a difficult grape for North American wineries, with the best results seen in cool, ocean-cleaned regions. Pinot Noir is one of the world's oldest *vinifera*, and with that age comes a certain amount of genetic instability. The vine is subject to frost damage, the grape clusters are prone to rot and sunburn, and disease can set rapidly. There are dozens upon dozens of clones and a winemaker's choice of a suitable clone version is critical, as is careful vineyard pruning technique and planting density. When all the factors line up, this grape produces a light- to medium-bodied, elegant, long-lived wine with bright cherry, raspberry, and earthy notes, pairing well with our local specialties like wild salmon, mushrooms, and Salt Spring lamb. And if you can't bear the heartbreak? Pinot Noir is an excellent grape for use in sparkling wines, which our island winemakers are increasingly producing.

Wild Cards

It's impossible to describe all of the rare and experimental grapes grown on the wine islands here—there are just too many! Below are a few exceptional wild cards and the wineries that are having success with them.

Agria [AG-ree-ah]
a.k.a.: Turan

This Hungarian varietal is often seen in the very dark, rustic, full-bodied reds of Eastern Europe. And its parents are as obscure to us as it is: Agria is a cross of Bikavar 8 (derived from Teinturier and Kadarka) and Gardonvi G (derived from Malbec and Perle de Csaba). On the islands, it is most often used in blends, to add colour and body—especially to our lighter Pinot Noir. Cherry Point Estate Wines vinifies it solely, however, in their big and brooding Bête Noir.

Black Muscat

a.k.a.: Golden Hamburg, Black Hamburg, Muscat de Hambourg, Moscato di Amburgo, Muscat Gamburgskiy, Hampton Court Vine, Queen's Arbor

As you can probably guess by the multilingual aliases above, this grape is grown globally—from North America to Russia to Italy to Greece to Russia to China. Black Muscat was created from the crossing of Schiava Grossa with Muscat of Alexandria. With the exception of California, where it is crafted into a popular dessert wine, it is generally made into a dry table wine, and usually found in blends. The grape is also used for eating out of hand, and is popular in fruit baskets from France. On the islands it is vinified as a single varietal by Blue Grouse Vineyards, resulting in an off-dry, aromatic light red.

Cayuga [kay-OO-guh]

Cayuga White is a North American cross of hybrids Schuyler and Seyval Blanc. As with all hybrids, it was created with a specific goal and thus planted here for its hardiness and disease-resistance nature. Cayuga wines have been said to be Riesling-like, with great fruit and bright acid. The grape is widely seen around the Finger Lakes region of New York State and in other spots in the eastern US. In BC, it is grown only by Vigneti Zanatta, and used for their flagship sparkling Fantasia.

Leon Millot [LAY-owhn MEE-yoh]

a.k.a.: Millot

This sister grape to islands' mainstay Marechal Foch (same cross) is known as *le médicin du vin* or "wine doctor" in Alsace, for its ability to darken the hue of Pinot Noir without a noticeable effect on the quality. Very similar to Foch, Leon Millot has more bright berry and fruit flavours and aromas. Salt Spring Vineyards' Millotage is a blend of Leon Millot with Marechal Foch, resulting in a lighter red with nice cherry and red berry flavours.

Madeleine Sylvaner [MAD-eh-layne sil-VAN-ner]

Madeleine Sylvaner is certainly a risky grape for the winemaker. True, it is aromatic, with delicate peach, apricot, and citrus notes. However, this early-ripening grape is highly susceptible to attack by rot, birds, and wasps. It is worth it? Certainly a number of our island winemakers think so. Though it is often used in blending for its sweet yet subtle fruit flavours, Venturi-Schulze Vineyards has made both single varietals of this grape and aromatic white blends.

Müller-Thurgau [MOO-ler TER-gow]

a.k.a.: Rivaner

This cool-climate-loving white hybrid grape is a German cross between Riesling and Chasselas. The goal was to combine Riesling's intensity and complexity with an early-ripening grape. By the 1970s, Müller-Thurgau had become Germany's most-planted grape, no doubt thanks to its ability to adapt to numerous climates and soil types. It is most often used as a blending wine, with floral, melon, and ripe pineapple flavours, and lower acid. Chase and Warren Estate Winery near Port Alberni uses it in their off-dry Beaufort Slope blend.

Zweigelt [ZVI-gelt]

a.k.a.: Rotburger, Zweigeltrebe

I love this quote from Jancis Robinson, a British wine writer and editor *of The Oxford Companion to Wine*: "The export fortunes of the variety may, oddly enough, be hampered by its originator's uncompromisingly Germanic surname. If only he had been called Dr. Pinot Noir." Zweigelt is a cross of St. Laurent and Blaufränkisch, created by Austrian Dr. Fritz Zweigelt. It is the most widely grown red grape in Austria, and its cold-hardiness, late bud break, and early ripening have been noticed by a few BC winemakers. Garry Oaks Winery was the first to bring it to the coast, and their lush, spicy, fruity Zeta is 100 percent estate-grown Zweigelt.

Blackberry dessert wines could be considered the signature wine of the region. Here, a lineup of the area's best await tasting at the Cowichan Wine & Culinary Festival.

BLACKBERRY DESSERT WINES

Treve Ring

In a region where blackberries are so rampantly abundant, it's no wonder they've made their way into our libations. One can only make so much blackberry jam after all. The rich, fertile soil and moist island air are the perfect conditions for these deeply flavoured berries, which are said to be "Mother Nature's gift" to the Cowichan First Nations people. Fortified blackberry wine has become somewhat synonymous with the islands, some calling it our namesake wine. Although people have called these blackberry wines "Port," and many are indeed port-style, the use of that name is protected by law in the European Union and is limited only to those wines from Portugal's Douro Valley. Sensitive winemakers have become creative with the nomenclature and avoid the use of the word: Averill Creek's Cowichan Black and Starling Lane's Port Victoria Wild Blackberry among them.

So what is blackberry dessert wine—and why do people stock up by the case and carefully pack it in their suitcases? Handpicked, ripe, late-summer berries are crafted into a luscious, potent, and heady sweet wine. With twice as many black-berries as a fruit table wine, these black beauties are certainly worth the sacrifice of the extra fruit. Some of these dessert wines are made in much the same way as classic Ports: the wine's fermentation is stopped with the addition of a grain spirit. Since fermentation is fuelled by sugar, this process leaves the wine's sugar levels high, resulting in a sweet final product. Other winemakers employ different yeasts that can handle higher alcohol levels, and only add sugar gradually until the yeast "stalls." Either way, the goal should be a balance between sweetness and acidity. Otherwise, we might as well just stick to jam.

Cherry Point Vineyards was the first to produce a blackberry dessert wine on a large scale. In 2001, after putting out a call for berries, they received approximately 5,000 pounds of local blackberries from friends and neighbours. In the last few years, that number has jumped to over 25,000 pounds of fruit—just to keep up with demand. With success like that, it's no wonder other winemakers were lured into making their own. Surprisingly, the styles range as much as grape wines do—from mildly sweet, bright fruit wine to intense, inky, and syrupy sippers.

Averill Creek's Cowichan Black is at the lighter end of this spectrum. It is naturally fermented to 16 percent alcohol, with a candied berry nose, sweet grapey and cherry flavours, and nice, vibrant acidity on the lengthy, satisfying, fruity finish. Salt Spring Vineyards Blackberry "Port" is also of the lighter, lively style, with the leafiness of the berry shining through, bright cherry and cassis notes, great acidity and lovely balance. Crafted from organic wild blackberries, it's another worthy choice for someone seeking a lighter style.

Rocky Creek Winery's Wild Blackberry's amazing aroma is a ringer for cocoa. Dusty, brambly cocoa, in fact, with sweet cassis and grapey notes and a medium body. This would also be a welcome addition in mixed cocktails or dessert recipes.

The veteran, Cherry Point's Cowichan Blackberry, has a dark, inky hue and a ripe blackberry nose. Peppery spice, leafy cedar flavours, and a drying finish make this suitable for pairing with savoury dishes. They also produce Blackberry Solera, by putting the former through the longer Solera aging process, resulting in a more elegant, smoother product. Carbrea Wild Blackberry Dessert Wine is much less sweet than the others. Full bodied (aided by their addition of Agria to the wine), with anise, cinnamon, and peppery spice, cooling menthol, and a dry finish, this is a post-dinner sipper for those without such a sweet tooth.

Beaufort puts a slightly different spin on things with their Black—a fortified wine using 10 percent blackcurrants, and the remainder local blackberries. With intense cassis nose and flavours, this wine has remarkable acidity and a depth reminiscent of unfiltered coffee and vanilla flavours. This one is aged in oak for up to 12 months.

Starling Lane Winery's Port Victoria Wild Blackberry wins the name game—and their dark, rich dessert wine easily wins fans, too. The most "port-like" of the bunch, it is rich and complex, with a currant aroma, flavours of dark chocolate and jammy berry, and a cool mint and vanilla finish that goes on and on. And Merridale Estate Cidery gets bonus points for distilling their own blackberry brandy to blend with island blackberries in their Mure Oh! A deep, rich, heady berry aroma and very Port-like nose lead to supple and smooth sweet, dark berry and cocoa flavours. The double hit of blackberries gives a great depth of flavours and a lengthy, spicy finish.

There are others not included here—and doubtless others in the making, just waiting to take advantage of our islands' prickly black beauties.

12 fresh figs
1 Tbsp (15 mL) granulated sugar
1 cup (250 mL) blackberry dessert wine
1 tsp (5 mL) chiffonaded basil
Pinch of sea salt
¼ lb (125 g) mascarpone cheese
¼ lb (125 g) cream cheese
3 egg whites (3 oz [90 mL])
1½ oz (45 g) granulated or raw sugar

BC Figs Poached in Blackberry Dessert Wine with Mascarpone Mousse

I came up with this late summer dessert recipe for using the many excellent blackberry dessert wines. Alternately, you could substitute any sweet dessert wine. Note: fresh figs are in season on the west coast in August and September. —Treve Ring

Destem the figs and make 2 small cuts to form a cross at the stem end of each one. Place the figs in a small saucepan. In a measuring cup, dissolve 1 Tbsp (15 mL) granulated sugar in the blackberry wine, and then pour over the figs. Add the basil and sea salt and allow to marinate for at least 1 hour. Meanwhile, allow the cheeses to come to room temperature.

Combine the egg whites and the 1½ oz (45 g) sugar in a bowl. Heat gently over barely simmering water and, using a hand-mixer, whip until the egg whites form medium-sized peaks of meringue.

Combine the cheeses in a bowl, stirring until smooth. Fold the meringue into the cheese mixture until evenly mixed, and then chill the mousse in the refrigerator, covered, for about 15 minutes.

Return the saucepan containing the figs to low heat and allow to come to a simmer. Poach the figs for about 5 minutes, depending on their ripeness. Carefully remove the figs from the wine and allow to cool slightly.

Increase the heat under the blackberry wine until the mixture begins to boil. Reduce by two-thirds, or until the liquid turns into a syrup.

Scoop a quarter of mousse onto a plate or into a glass. Top each serving with 2 to 3 figs and a drizzle of syrup.

Serves 4

BLATTNERS
Treve Ring

In the wine world, the term "hybrid" indicates that two or more vine growths of different species have been crossed genetically to produce a new species. The purpose is to combine the best characteristics of the parent vines while eliminating their weaknesses. This is done by human intervention, unlike naturally evolved vines, and doesn't involve any genetic modification, which many consumers are against. Many of the hybrids were created as a response to seasonal temperature extremes and to counter various diseases that can affect the vines.

A Swiss scientist, Valentin Blattner, began breeding grapes in the 1980s with the aim of finding disease-resistant, commercially viable grapes for wine production. Blattner crossed noble *vinifera* varieties with other subspecies. In the mid-1990s some of his varieties were grown in the northern Okanagan and subsequently brought to the west coast. For the past ten years, several growers have been involved in trials here with those varieties, along with some others that Blattner and well-known and respected Victoria-based winemaker Paul Troop brought here. These vines are often referred to as "Blattners," "Blattner crosses," and "Swiss varietals." Commercial production of the early selections has yielded wines from Roger Dosman's Alderlea Vineyards as well as Salt Spring Vineyards, where Troop is winemaker. A 2008 BC Wine Institute survey listed 42.5 acres each of Blattner whites and reds grown in BC. In 2010 and 2011 a number of wineries should be releasing wines from these grapes.

The first vine selected has become known as Cabernet Foch, giving some clue to its parentage. It produces dark, densely flavoured wines with nuances of chocolate, tobacco, and cassis (Alderlea's Fusion is Cabernet Foch). Since then, Troop, Dosman, and others have selected another red, Cabernet Libre, with a Loire-like Cabernet Franc style, and two whites: Petite Milo, with flavours ranging from

A look at the future? This Blattner cross numbered variety 48.05.83. may be one of the best reds for this region. It ripens well, produces a good crop, and makes wine with good notes of cassis and blackberry.

Sancerre to Riesling depending on ripeness and winemaking, and Epicure, unique in its flavour but leaning toward a big fruity wine, but without the floral qualities of many of the German crosses.

There are several very promising varieties that will be available over the next few years, and many more that need to be tried in the Okanagan as they ripen too late for this region.

According to Troop, these vines represent a major step forward for the coastal region. "They combine high levels of disease resistance with commercially viable crops, and wine that is outstanding in ways that the traditional varieties grown in this area seldom match. For the grower, it means lower costs and less chemical usage. For the winery, it is a chance to work with grapes that, while not *vinifera*, taste very European. This opens the door for the creation of a unique regional wine identity."

FRUIT WINES

Treve Ring

Poor fruit wines. Disregarded by many as homemade concoctions, a step away from vinegar, or a syrupy glog. "Oh no, I don't like sweet wines," "That stuff gives me a headache," "My uncle used to make cherry wine in the basement—made me sick!" Perhaps that used to be the case, but the commercial fruit wines of today have grown up—especially in Canada. Winemakers are tending to fruit wines with the care and passion needed for grape wines. Don't forget—grapes are also fruit, after all, and why should just one fruit have the glory of bacchanalian celebrations? Why limit ourselves, especially with the hundreds of fruits out there?

Canada is a major player in the fruit wine world, along with Germany, Austria, the UK, New Zealand, and the US. There are over 60 fruit wineries in Canada, with every province producing fruit wines (thus far). Contrary to popular belief, fruit wines are not always sweet. Many could pass as a traditional grape varietal in any blind tasting. They are vinified much as grape wines are but with the added benefit of being quicker and more economical to produce. Just as with grape-wine making, the flesh is separated from the peel or skin by machine or, more likely, by hand. The pulp is crushed into liquid and the seeds and skins are skimmed or spun off. The liquid is then put into a fermentation vessel and yeast is added, initiating the fermentation process. The maturation period is much shorter for fruit wines than for grape wines (one to six months as compared to eight to 24 months), freeing up much needed space in the winery and allowing for quick turnaround time.

In addition, fruit wineries have the benefit of multiple harvests throughout the year, as the ripening period for each fruit varies. As with grape wines, the winemaker can also add his or her own techniques to the procedure. Depending on their modus operandi, the wine may or may not see time in oak barrels or undergo malolactic fermentation, in addition to other traditional grape vinification techniques. The vintner can also use frozen fruit in many cases without sacrificing the quality of the final product. Most likely, the vintner will be trying to capture the vibrancy of the fruit—the vast majority of fruit wines are meant to be drunk young.

In hopes of replacing the Vintners Quality Assurance (VQA), which doesn't currently recognize fruit wines in their program, fruit wineries tried to assemble their own national association of producers: Fruit Wines of Canada, or FWC. Unfortunately, the nationwide organization never got off the ground, but they were able to establish Quality Certified (QC) standards that outline regulations regarding production, packaging, labelling, and testing. In order to be certified QC, a wine must be made from a list of recognized fruit species (no grapes allowed) and from 100 percent fruit from the region specified. Similar to the VQA, the fruit wine must also be evaluated by a qualified tasting panel, which must deem it free of faults. Because of these policies and others, and also like the VQA, the QC program has its promoters and detractors. Regardless, there is a busy Fruit Wines of Ontario chapter that was established in 1998. The Ontario group has been successful in obtaining grants from both federal and provincial governments to assist in establishing, lobbying, and marketing the industry. Their long-term goal is to establish a reputation and following for their products internationally.

One way to get the word out is via the awards circuit. In addition to the Fruit Wines of Canada National Awards, fruit wines are awarded and celebrated on such important stages as The All Canadian Wine Championships (canadianwinetrail.com), the Canadian Wine Awards (wineaccess.ca), the Northwest Wine Summit (vinochallenge.com), and the Vino Awards (rockymountainwine.com), among others.

It's not just our eastern cousins that are fruit forward; the fruit wine industry is booming business in BC as well. Some wines are bone dry, with serious tannins and colour. Others are sticky sweet, long-legged, and unctuous. Most hover somewhere in the middle—off dry, fruit forward, and food friendly (see sidebar on page 130).

And with the islands' incredible abundance of wild blackberries, it's no wonder that the majority of our fruit wines make use of them—we've made a name for ourselves for our blackberry port-style wines. There are other fruits, however: blueberries, currants, gooseberries, cranberries, pear, apple, raspberry, quince, rhubarb, and kiwi.

Merridale Estate Cidery has taken their fruited production one step further, with the addition of their Brandihouse in 2007 and the crafting of eaux-de-vie and fortified apple and grape brandies.

Talk about *terroir*—just as you can taste the islands in our grape wines, the orchards and berry bushes come through in our fruit wines as well. If we can overcome the stigma of homemade syrupy concoctions, this all-but-hidden industry will truly blossom.

OTHER FRUIT WINERIES

MooBerry Winery
Proprietor: Phil Charlebois
403 Lowry's Road, Parksville
Open to the Public: Yes (check website for hours)
Products/Wines: Fruit Wines: Apple, Pear, Cherry, Gooseberry, Raspberry, Blackberry, Blueberry, Blackberry Dessert, Cherry Dessert
T: 250-954-3931 | TF: 1-877-248-4353 | W: mooberrywinery.com
Comments: All wines are made from BC fruit, some island-grown. The winery is located at Morningstar Farm (also home to Little Qualicum Cheeseworks).

Silverside Farm & Winery

Proprietors: Don Bull and Lyn Jakimchuk

3810 Cobble Hill Road, Cobble Hill

Open to the Public: Yes (check website for hours)

Products/Wines: Wild Blackberry Wine, Wild Blackberry Port, Blueberry Port, Tayberry Wine, Raspberry Wine, Raspberry Port

T: 250-743-9149 | TF: 1-877-743-9149;

E: info@silversidefarm.com | W: silversidefarm.com

Comments: As its name indicates, Silverside is both a farm and a winery. In addition to the fruit wines made here, visitors can also buy local produce and berries (in season).

Fruit Wine and Food Pairing Primer

Contrary to popular belief, not all fruit wines are crafted to pair with desserts. Here are both savoury and sweet matches to make.

Table Wines

Apple—cheese fondue, pork, poultry, hazelnuts

Blackberry—sponge cake, biscotti, soft cheeses

Black Currant—lamb, beef

Blueberry—pork, duck, pate

Cranberry—turkey, pork, pasta dishes

Kiwi—curries, Thai, Jamaican cuisines

Loganberry—duck, flat breads, soft cheese, pecans

Peach—shellfish, seafood, salads

Pear—Brie, pecans, spinach, creamy pasta dishes

Quince—pear cobbler, tarte tatin

Raspberry—spinach, pecans, blue cheeses, dark chocolate

Rhubarb—Mexican cuisines, cilantro, strawberry crumble

Strawberry—salads

Late Harvest Wines

Apple—apple pie, raisin tarts, sharp cheddar

Apricot/Peach—carrot cake, lemon meringue, angel food cake, crème caramel

Blackberry—cheeses, chocolate, walnuts, vanilla ice cream

Blueberry—cheesecake, vanilla ice cream

Cherry—dark chocolate, cheesecake

Pumpkin—pumpkin pie, ginger ice cream, pecan tart, gingersnaps

Raspberry—dark chocolate, truffles

SPARKLING WINES

Treve Ring

It's *the* special occasion wine—almost any anniversary, holiday, wedding or retirement will feature a bottle of obligatory bubbly (or bubble, as sparkling wine is sometimes called). Of course, buying French Champagne is easy—except on the pocketbook. Our local BC bubbly is almost always crafted in the same painstaking *méthode traditionnelle* (traditional method) that authentic Champagne is—with prices as easy to swallow as the wine itself. And despite the complicated production and hands-on time required, more and more winemakers are trying their hands at capturing festivities in a glass. Well-made locally produced sparkling? Suddenly, any day ending in Y is a perfect excuse to break out the bubbly.

Though any grape can be made into sparkling wine, the most suitable ones are those with higher acid and lower sugar levels—both key characteristics of our islands' wines. The higher acidity provides a lively and crisp-finished product, and the lower sugar levels help keep the final alcohol level appropriately balanced after the second fermentation is complete.

Second fermentation? That's correct—it is part of the process that creates those magic bubbles. Sparkling wine begins in the same way as any wine, with the initial fermentation converting the natural sugar in the grapes into alcohol while the resultant carbon dioxide is allowed to escape. This base wine is then blended, or assembled, into a cuvée (or blended wine), if desired. In the traditional method, the second fermentation occurs in each individual bottle: more sugar and yeast are added, starting another fermentation process. This time, however, the bottle is sealed tight with a crown cap so the carbon dioxide has no chance to escape. Instead, the gas slowly melds with the wine under pressure in the bottle (which can reach up to seven times atmospheric pressure). When this second fermentation is complete, and the wine has rested on the lees (spent yeast cells) for a minimum of

18 months, the crown cap is popped, the plug of yeast cells is disgorged, the wine is topped up with *dosage* (to replace what shot out with the plug) and the bottle is sealed.

There are still many variations on this lengthy process—from what grapes will be selected and at what ripeness they are harvested, to the winery's cuvée, to how long the fermentation is left to take place, to what will comprise the dosage, to what sort of closure is selected. There's a style for everyone. Island vintners are creating sparklers that range from crisp, delicate, floral, and citrus to richer, full-bodied, toasty wines. Here is a look at who is making magic in the bottle.

Vigneti Zanatta leads the field in sparkling wines, with a third of their production and up to six different bubblies in their portfolio at any one time. Some are made in quite limited quantities, but all are handcrafted in the traditional method, save for the *frizzante* Damasco.

Their flagship bubbly, Glenora Fantasia Brut, is crafted from Cayuga grapes and aged for a minimum of three years, producing a Granny Smith-crisp, green-apple-kissed sparkler. Brut Tradizionale is their newest offering, and their closest to traditional French Champagne in style. Rich and full bodied, it is made from Pinot Noir and Chardonnay. Fatima Brut is crafted from Pinot Gris, and has delicate pear, clay, and mineral flavours. Allegria Brut Rosé is a strawberry-hued sparkling wine from Pinot Noir and Auxerrois grapes, with minted raspberry and blueberry flavours, and a more structured mouthfeel. Taglio Rosso Brut is also red—deeper crimson in colour—and crafted from Cabernet Sauvignon and Castel grapes. It is quite fruity, with raspberry and blackberry aromas and flavours. Their very popular Damasco is a blend of at least four grapes (with a mainstay of Auxerrois) to produce a light, fresh, slightly effervescent wine.

Venturi-Schulze Vineyards has made a number of sparkling wines over the years depending on the vintage and grapes at hand. Their mainstay sparkler, Brut Naturel, is a true island classic: a cuvée of Pinot Auxerrois, Pinot Gris and Kerner,

this sings of crisp citrus and toasted almonds. Lovely fine mousse and a crisp lemon finish.

Starling Lane Winery's Célébration Brut has such a keen following that it sells out in advance of its release. Pinot Noir and Chardonnay are blended to create a beautiful, medium-bodied bubbly with fresh lemon and strawberry aromas, and bright grapefruit, lime, and floral flavours.

Rocky Creek Winery's Katherine's Sparkle Brut is a fresh bubbly made from Ortega, Gewürztraminer, and Bacchus. Reminiscent of German Sekt, with bright peach and candied pear aromas, and green-apple and floral muscat flavours with big creamy mousse.

Salt Spring Vineyards' Karma is another blink-and-it's-sold-out favourite. A Pinot Noir and Chardonnay cuvée of bright mineral, citrus, and bready aromas, with crisp lime, lemon, and pear flavours, and a lovely, lengthy, lemon-zest finish.

Beaufort Winery Vineyard also released their first sparkling in 2010—a rosé crafted from Pinot Noir—which was not yet ready to sample as of deadline.

MEAD

Jeff Bateman

Buzz: as trend-watchers worth their weight in iPods will confirm, it's critical for any enterprise. Well, the buzz is loud and literal at Tugwell Creek Honey Farm and Meadery, a dozen or so wiggles of West Coast Road beyond Sooke. Hundreds of thousands of docile honeybees reside here along with owner/operators Bob Liptrot and Dana LeComte, their seven- and five-year-old daughters, Teagan and Sadie, two goats, the resident cat, Ootak, and, from time to time, an eager assistant from the Canadian SOIL apprenticeship program.

Collectively, this menagerie is making a joyous noise indeed. And why not? Six years after securing a licence as British Columbia's first meadery, Liptrot and LeComte are running a promising farm-gate business split evenly between sales of connoisseur-grade honey and their award-winning batches of mead, the honeyed nectar that has been intoxicating humans since prehistoric times. Tugwell Creek's limited-edition offerings are available at Sooke Harbour House and Markus' Wharfside Restaurant in Sooke, and Lure, and The Mark in Victoria, while bottles can be purchased at most Victoria wine stores, including the Spinnakers Brewpub wine store, Liberty Wine Merchants in Vancouver, and via e-mail order.

It's at Tugwell Creek's 12-acre Otter Point farm overlooking the Strait of Juan de Fuca, however, that the bulk of sales are made to day trippers compelled by the same kind of sweet tooth that hooked Liptrot on honey as a boy. A neighbour in East Vancouver kept a beehive and, in exchange for honeycomb, Liptrot became his helper and apprentice. After earning a Master's degree in entomology (the study of insects), he spent 15 years on staff at Vancouver's Mountain Equipment Co-op before he and LeComte, a fashion-industry veteran, chucked city life and followed their beekeeping dream to Vancouver Island.

That was 12 years ago, and the outdoorsy Liptrot loves the work despite the occupational hazards (he estimates his annual sting count at about 100). Each spring, some 100 colonies—which at their peak population will hold 50,000 residents apiece—are on the property under Liptrot's stewardship. By June, when the traffic gets busy along the narrow lane leading to their picturesque shop-cum-home, most will have been relocated to prime foraging areas elsewhere.

"Here, we're a little too close to the ocean and the weather can get nasty," says Liptrot. "The bees won't fly when it's wet, of course, and the flowers don't produce nectar." Many colonies are moved to forestry lands farther inland, where the bees sup on the fireweed and wildflowers that flourish in clearcuts. An apiary at the Sooke Potholes offers a feast of blackberry flowers, while a precious few hundred kilos of rare linden tree honey are sometimes harvested from Tugwell Creek's queen-bee mating facility at nearby Malahat Farm. Within the BC beekeeping community, Liptrot is known as "the toughest beekeeper on Vancouver Island," due to his success at his faraway location. Liptrot and his breeding bees are much in demand.

LeComte, who handles the marketing side of the operation, figures that exotic varietals (fireweed, arbutus, and salal flowers also produce distinctive honeys) are transforming beekeeping into a truly specialized art form. Vancouver Island honey is known for its lightness and floral attributes. Certainly, Tugwell Creek's honey is a far cry from the "Canada No. 1" uniformity achieved by mass-market producers. "You might as well be buying corn syrup," she laughs. "To heat and pasteurize honey is to take away its natural flavour."

The storeroom behind the farmhouse is filled with gleaming, stainless steel extractors, pumps, and processors. Beginning with the season's first harvests in late July, this gear removes raw honey from the comb and filters it down into the thick, head-spinningly tasty liquid gold sold in the shop and at local resorts like Point No Point. A portion of the 3,000 kilos of honey turned out annually is diverted to mead production, which requires its own set of distillation equipment and an adjacent cold room lined with French oak barrels.

Beekeepers have traditionally made mead for themselves by simply mixing water with the waxy "cappings" skimmed from the surface of honey in the early

stages of production. "We take it rather more seriously than that," says Liptrot, essentially the only professional meadmaker west of Ontario and one of about 100 worldwide. "Our goal is to construct full-bodied, full-flavoured meads using traditional methods."

To prove the point, he twists a spigot and pours a draft of spiced Metheglin. A dry mead with a pleasing thickness on the tongue, it's accented with hints of cinnamon, nutmeg, and cardamom. The surprise is that it's not at all sweet. "Yes, everyone expects mead to be sweet," says Liptrot, "but we personally don't like sweet wines." Demand for a traditional dessert wine is such, however, that small quantities of a fortified vintage Sack Mead are available from time to time and there is a waiting list.

As for a "signature mead," Tugwell Creek is producing a berry-flavoured Melomel (12 percent alcohol) on an annual basis. "It's a light sipping wine for the patio, not too intimidating, and something that people who have never experienced mead can ease into," says LeComte. "We used loganberries in this case to give it a little colour and dimension, but the berry will change each year and include marion-, logan- and gooseberries, and that should add to the appeal." For the meat lover, Tugwell produces a red mead that pairs with food the way a good red wine does. Called Kickass Currant Family Reserve, this mead is produced with the addition of blackcurrants, which give colour and add structure and tannins.

Mead ages superbly, notes Liptrot, and he points to its historic role as a lubricant for all manner of ceremonies. "It's like a good Port or Madeira in that it only gets better with age. People can leave a bottle in the cellar for ten years, then open it on a wedding anniversary."

Tugwell Creek's meads are produced in small batches, reflecting both uncertain public demand and the wholly realistic ambitions of the owners. "Who knows where this will end up, but we do want to keep things manageable," says LeComte as she gets ready to drive Teagan to school. "Our plan is to cover the bills, have a holiday once a year, and enjoy life." With the gentle hum of their bees as the soundtrack, it's a honey of a game plan.

Tugwell Creek Honey Farm and Meadery

Open to the Public: Yes (check website for hours)
8750 West Coast Road, Sooke
T: 250-642-1956 | W: tugwellcreekfarm.com
To learn more about mead, visit www.gotmead.com.

ANOTHER MEADERY

Middle Mountain Mead

Proprietors: Helen Grond and Stephen McGrath
3505 Euston Road, Hornby Island
Open to the Public: Yes (check website for hours)
Products/Wines: 11 different varieties of honey wine, flavoured with fruits, herbs, and botanicals
T: 250-335-1397 | E: meadmaker@middlemountainmead.com | W: middlemountainmead.com
Comments: This Hornby Island meadery is located on a farm that grows lavender, apples, blackcurrants and grapes—all ingredients they use in their mead. There are, of course, beehives as well that help provide the honey for the traditional honey wine.

CIDER
Treve Ring

Kingston Black, Chisel Jersey, Kings, Tremlett's Bitter, Michelin, Frequin Rouge, Hauxapfel. These names don't roll off the tongue as easily as Granny Smith or McIntosh. But they are all the same fruit: apples. Difference is, the former are cider apples and aren't anything that you'd want to bite into for a snack.

All of these apples, plus many more, are grown on Vancouver Island and crafted into traditional English cider. If you're wondering what exactly that is, you're not alone. Cider, like wine, is a fermented beverage but, unlike wine, the fruit used is apples, not grapes. Found in many parts of the world, cider was popular in North America until it was crushed by Prohibition, with most of the older cider orchards not surviving the ban. That's where Merridale Estate Cidery in Cobble Hill and Sea Cider Farm & Ciderhouse in Saanichton are making their mark, educating consumers one at a time. Both ciderhouses are culinary tourism mainstays—places where thirsty travellers can come and taste a cider lineup, enjoy food pairings, take a tour, revel in the orchard view and—importantly—learn a bit about authentic artisan ciders.

Cider apples are grouped into four main types, according to the nature of their flavour components.

Sweets contain high sugar levels, which encourage fermentation and raise the final alcohol levels. This group is low in tannins and acidity.

Sharps are high in acidity and add "bite" to the cider. They tend to be low in sugar and have little tannin.

Bittersweets are high in sugar but also contain raised levels of tannin, which tastes bitter and is astringent. A certain amount of bitterness is expected in all but the sweetest ciders.

Bittersharps are high in both tannins and fruit acids.

The fall harvest is pressed and turned into juice, fermented with yeast, and aged into a complex and crisp alcoholic beverage. Much like wine, ciders are typically blended, using juice from several apples to give the best results. These results range from a light, slightly fizzy Prosecco-style to full, dry, wood-aged ciders suitable for accompanying a meaty meal. And, of course, befitting our islands' experimental nature, the apples have also been crafted into rich, fortified, sweet sippers.

Merridale Estate Cidery owners Janet Docherty and Rick Pipes are local culinary tourism icons, tireless wine industry supporters, and highly respected entrepreneurs. In addition to the Ciderhouse, where they handcraft a lineup of traditional ciders, they have the Brandihouse (the site of their distillery and a stunning showcase of production), Bistro la Pommeraie (a locally based bistro focused on their impressive brick oven), plus the Merridale Spa. Knowing little about cider when they purchased the business in 2000, they were quick learners and forward thinkers, speedily mastering the techniques and creating packaging to make cider appealing to the uninitiated. Their 13 acres are planted with approximately 18 varieties of apples. Merridale Ciders are packaged in recyclable plastic bottles.

Their Traditional Cider is aptly named—and the closest to traditional English cider in style—clean, crisp, dry, and slightly effervescent with flavours of green apples and fresh green grass. House Cider is a little more public-pleasing—slightly sweeter and lighter, but still dry. Scrumpy, named for an English cider made by farm workers who stole or "scrumped" apples from orchards, is sharp, strong, and very dry, with a clean apple finish. For those who prefer something a little sweeter, they have Cyser—kissed with wildflower honey—and Merri Berri—strawberry-hued from blending with local berries. Cidre Normandie is a still cider, oak-aged for extra depth and complexity, and Champagne Style Somerset is a dry sparkling cider, ready for toasting occasions. And for dessert, Winter Apple is a rich, brown-sugar-and-butterscotch sweet delight.

Fresh aromas of baked apples and buttery brown sugar. Merridale Estate Cidery's Winter Apple Cider.

Sea Cider's Wild English is fermented with wild yeast and organic English bittersweet cider apples. It is a dry, earthy, and powerful cider in the Herefordshire style.

Sea Cider Farm & Ciderhouse is owned and operated Kristen and Bruce Jordan, who spent three years planting 1,000 organic apple trees—comprising some 50 varieties—on ten acres of the Saanich Peninsula, plus painstakingly building a stunning ciderhouse onsite. The property has a full view of both the Gulf Islands and their orchard, and houses the entire cider-making process—from growing to milling, pressing, fermenting, and bottling. Since opening in 2007, Sea Cider has become a local beacon for culinary tourism and both Kristen and Bruce are heavily involved in their community. Sociability, sustainability, and community involvement are the three pillars of Sea Cider's business philosophy.

Flagship is just that—and for good reason. Super-slow fermentation has yielded an extra-dry crisp cider with hints of anise and other spices. Wild English gives a clue to its method—this dry sparkler is fermented with wild yeast from the apple skins, giving a distinctive earthy flavour. Kings & Spies, Sea Cider's only non-organic cider, is slightly effervescent, yet creamy in the mouth—crafted primarily from King and Northern Spy apples grown in Victoria backyards. The proceeds from Kings & Spies support LifeCycles, a local organization that promotes food education. Pippins is a crisp and aromatic cider redolent of dried apricot notes. Rumrunner is darker in hue, coloured through aging in rum barrels. Hints of quince, brown sugar, and exotic spice, and a fuller body are hallmarks of this complex, semi-dry sparkling cider. If you prefer more sweetness, try Cyser—heritage apples are blended with fermented organic honey, resulting in rich flavours of lemon and honeysuckle. Pommeau is a still, aperitif-style cider crafted from Snow apples, whose Normandy origins date to the 1600s. Silken smooth, with velvety mouthfeel and focussed flavours of baked apple and caramelized sugar. And for their cider take on BC's iconic icewine? Pomona is made from frozen crabapples, whose juice is slowly cool-fermented, yielding a rich, citrus, and crème caramel honeyed elixir.

Their ciders are sold in hefty, traditional, flip-top ginger beer flasks.

Merridale Estate Cidery
Open to the Public: Yes (check website for hours)
1230 Merridale Road, Cobble Hill
T: 250-743-4293
TF: 1-800-998-9908
W: merridalecider.com

Sea Cider Farm & Ciderhouse
Open to the Public: Yes (check website for hours)
2487 Mt. St. Michael Road, Saanichton
T: 250-544-4824
W: seacider.ca

ARTISAN DISTILLERS

Treve Ring

What exactly is distilling? Distilling is a concentrating technique, taking a lighter strength alcoholic solution to a higher strength alcoholic solution. Anything is distillable, as long as one can convert the inherent natural sugars to alcohol through fermentation. Once a product has fermented to an alcoholic state, it is carefully heated to precise temperatures, releasing the prized alcoholic congeners or flavouring vapours. These vapours are collected, cooled, and liquefied, and only the heart—or purest part—is kept for the spirits. These selected liquids are then set to rest in stainless steel (for freshness) or casks (for maturation), depending on the desired result, and left to age until they are determined to be ready.

So you've distilled your product and are ready to market and sell it. Not so fast—spirits are a whole different game here in British Columbia. This brand-new industry faces much the same problems that small farm-gate wineries faced in the 1970s: obtaining recognition and credibility from the government, and having taxation and sale laws that allow a producer to make a profit. The only distilling rules in place were set decades ago, and were aimed at the large, mega-producing Canadian spirit giants capable of producing many millions of litres each year. As it stands now, distillers have to turn over their product to the British Columbia Liquor Distribution Branch (BCLDB), only to have it "consigned back" for sale. Hardly a profitable business model. The Ministries of Agriculture, Tourism, and Small Business are supportive of changes to the liquor laws, as they will increase agricultural tourism, but such changes take time—even years. (Hmm, much like a fine aged whisky . . .)

The Artisan Distillers Guild of BC is a united voice for small distilleries—an attempt at a critical mass tipping point, if you will. Since its inception in 2007, the group has worked to set up guidelines for membership, to promote the use of

BC agricultural products, and to differentiate themselves from the giant distillate companies. A minimum of 95 percent of the base spirit has to be from BC, and the creators have to distill the product themselves. Much like BC's small wineries, each has its own special characteristics and nuances. And the agritourism market will benefit from distillers being able to hand sell their products at the place of creation. The consumer benefits, the producer benefits—perhaps the BCLDB is the only one that doesn't benefit.

Victoria Spirits

Begun by veteran winemaker Ken Winchester and his business partner, Bryan Murray, Victoria Gin is a true local success story and reflective of the high quality of spirit produced here. Recognized and revered across North America, Victoria Gin blends 11 botanicals (one of which is a closely guarded and hotly coveted secret) into an aromatic, smooth, and complex spirit. This classic is rightly known as Canada's first premium gin. Winchester later departed the alcohol industry, leaving Victoria Spirits to be run by Murray. Distilling is overseen by Peter Hunt. After a year or so of scrambling to keep up with demand for Victoria Gin, they have started once again to investigate new products. Their biggest focus has been for a completely local, single-malt whisky (preliminarily named Craigdarroch Whisky), which should be ready for consumption in 2013. Their Twisted & Bitter orange bitters has been embraced by local mixologists, the new Left Coast Hemp Vodka is sure to be a huge hit in BC, and they are also creating grappas here and there as time allows.

Merridale Estate Cidery—The Brandiworks

Adding to the critical mass is Rick Pipes, owner of the Cowichan Valley's Merridale Cider. After years of studying the art of traditional cider-making and fruit, he turned his hand to fruit brandy and eaux de vies. Merridale Brandiworks opened in 2007 with a release of two eaux de vie, one made from blackberries and the other from Merridale's own cider apples.

They've also crafted two fortified dessert-style beverages made with Merridale's own brandies. The Pomme Oh is made in the tradition of the finest *pommeaux* from Normandy, with freshly picked French cider apples pressed into juice. The juice begins to ferment in French oak barrels, and then, at the perfect balance of sweetness, the fermentation is stopped by the addition of earlier produced Apple Oh de Vie. The Mure Oh is made by a similar process with blackberries, but in stainless steel vats to preserve the delicate fruit aroma of the blackberry. "We are very excited to be the first winery on the island to be using our own brandy in our sweet fortified wines. It allows us to truly express the flavour of the Cowichan Valley fruit," says Pipes. Most other fortified products in BC are made with neutral grain alcohol because it is cheaper and readily available. "It takes more time and is more costly to use brandy from local fruit, but we believe it is a better-tasting product."

Island Spirits Distillery

Hornby Island's Island Spirits Distillery is the little Phrog that could. A foundation of three partners gave way to two in early 2010 with the departure of winemaker John Grayson, and it is now run by icebreaker captain and distiller Pete Kimmerly and professor of organic chemistry Naz Abdurahman. Nothing in the spirit world starts quickly—the first products were painstakingly crafted using a still of their own creation (20 years in the making!). Their goal is purity—so much so that their ultra premium spirits are said to cause no hangovers and trigger no allergies. Distilling is part science, part art, part skill, and many parts patience. Island Spirits started with Phrog Gin and Phrog Vodka. To avoid the BC liquor system, almost all of their product was sent to Alberta for sale. There, the privatized liquor distribution system is a much friendlier business model for artisan distillers, and response to Island Spirits has been overwhelmingly positive. Plans for 2010 included adding Vanilla Vodka, Black Jelly Bean Sichuan Vodka, and a nice Anise, Fennel, Cumin Aquavit to the lineup, along with a revamped website.

Shelter Point Distillery

The grandest distillery on the island has had the grandest delays of them all. Nearly five years in the planning, partners Jay Oddleifson, Patrick Evans, and Andrew Currie's campaign for a malt whisky distillery in the Comox Valley had to pass some major hurdles from the local government and face the economic reality of the latter part of the decade. But having Lagavulin master distiller Mike Nicholson on board lends credibility and experience to this project. Shelter Point Distillery is approximately 8,000 square feet, designed to contain the still and room for up to 3,000 barrels. Crop trials for barley on the property, located within the Agricultural Land Reserve, look promising, and the next step is to design a new machine to process the malt—and learn the skill of malting. Nicholson's aim is to grow the barley, malt then distill it, and age it onsite—with a goal of 25,000 litres per year. Shelter Point Farm also produces around one million pounds of raspberries annually so chances are good a raspberry liqueur will be one of the first products available.

FUTURE UP-AND-COMERS

Matt Phillips

Another founding member of the Artisan Distillers Guild of BC is local brewmaster Matt Phillips. Though most will know him through his very popular Phillips Brewing Company, the extremely creative and mechanically inclined Phillips has built his own still from scratch. Unlike the more commonly used copper pot still, Phillips' is stainless and steam-fired, and it can hold up to 22 different plates—useful for infusing spirits with various flavours. It lends itself very well to gin, which is a compounded spirit made with the addition of flavouring compounds, usually botanicals. If and when Phillips has time away from making delicious beer, we're going to have some serious gin on our hands.

Maxwell James Spirits

As my deadline approached, intriguing details were developing about a new company. A well-connected and popular mix-master named Maxwell James has incorporated Maxwell James Spirits. There's a website holding space, a Facebook group full of hipster well-wishers and tasting volunteers, and he has fashioned his entire setup of handmade equipment with an enthusiast buddy. News came out about the collaborations in the works—James is planning his whisky with friends who own a brewery, he's working on a coffee liqueur with product from a local roastery, and he's talking with Okanagan coopers to locate the perfect barrels for his needs. His opening acts will be a gin and a pair of rums (white and spiced). And he has crafted "a marketing campaign that includes fictional characters associated with each product . . . their tales are woven together into a massive story and illustrated in a graphic novel/comic book." I am looking forward to delving into the MJS Chronicles over the coming years.

Island Spirits Distillery

4605 Roburn Road, Hornby Island
T: 250-335-0630
W: islandspirits.ca

Matt Phillips

2010 Government Street, Victoria
T: 250-380-1912
W: phillipsbeer.com

Maxwell James Spirits

W: mjspirits.com
twitter.com/MJSpirits

Merridale Estate Cidery—The Brandiworks

1230 Merridale Road, Cobble Hill
T: 250-743-4293 TF: 1-800-998-9908
W: merridalecider.com

Shelter Point Distillery

W: shelterpointdistillery.com

Victoria Spirits

6170 Old West Saanich Road, Saanich
T: 250-544-8217
W: victoriaspirits.com

CRAFT BEER

Adem Tepedelen

Given Victoria's distinctly English influence, it's not surprising that Canada's first in-house brewpub opened here in 1984, long before island wineries were up and running. That brewpub, Spinnakers, is still an integral part of the thriving craft beer scene and, yes, their beers—a great assortment of classic ales from hopped-up IPAs to black-as-night imperial stouts—and the atmosphere of their harbourside location remain very English-influenced.

Geographically, Vancouver Island and the Gulf Islands are close to one of the United States' premier beer cities, Seattle, but the brew culture is distinctive. Local brewers have certainly been influenced by the pervasive west coast style, in which aromatic hops are used in abundance, but the local palate has long favoured more malt-leaning styles such as amber ales, pale ales, nut brown ales, cream ales, and other similar varieties. That's only slowly starting to change, as brewers have begun to take more chances and are finding a receptive market for their bolder flavours.

Though, as we'll see, there is great craft beer being made in numerous places on the islands, Victoria remains ground zero for anyone interested in exploring the beer scene here. Two of the three well-established brewpubs are right downtown—Canoe and Swans—and Spinnakers is a short walk across the famous blue Johnson Street bridge (after which Spinnakers has named their double IPA). Canoe's waterfront location and outdoor patio make it ideal for enjoying one of their thirst-quenching ales on a warm, sunny afternoon. Their selection is somewhat modest—lager, bitter, brown ale, pale ale—but all are well made. Their seasonal wheat beer is a perfect patio quaffer. About a block away, Swans offers a larger, more varied selection of brews (as well as an attached liquor store where you can buy chilled bottles of their beers to take with you) in their historic old building.

Their raspberry ale is a refreshing, well-balanced stand-out. Tours of the brewery are also offered.

Island residents love to support island businesses, which is why the four local craft breweries do so well here. Though they vary in size and approach, all have their fans and all have found the Victoria area very eager to embrace fresh, small-batch beers.

Vancouver Island Brewery is the largest of the four and though their impressive facility on Government Street wouldn't seem to make small-batch brews, compared to macrobreweries like Molson and Labatt, it's positively quaint. Their standard selection of beers—lager, pale ale, honey brown ale, dark lager—is mostly on the typical, conservative side, but their limited-edition winter seasonal, a nearly 10 percent ABV eisbock, is a hearty, complex winter warmer that sells out in a hurry.

Most of Lighthouse Brewing's offerings—lager, pale ale, amber ale, IPA, and stout—are available in cans only, but they have also started bottling a few of their selections (the super-popular Race Rocks Amber and newer Riptide Pale Ale and Fisgard 150). If you're not a fan of canned beers, you'll have no trouble finding Lighthouse beers on draught at most bars in town.

The two newer and more adventurous breweries in Victoria are Phillips and Driftwood; both are well distributed in the Victoria area and even at some more discerning pubs and restaurants on the mainland. Phillips actually preceded Driftwood by a few years and, as such, they have a much bigger presence in the Victoria beer scene. Their standard line-up—IPA, lager, amber ale, cream ale, Belgian trippel, porter, double IPA, India dark ale—is anything but standard and they generally crank out an interesting new seasonal brew every couple of months. The Driftwood guys must have taken a cue from Phillips' example in that they, too, have put together a lineup—pale ale, altbier, witbier, saison, and IPA—that's certainly not predictable. They also offer a host of intriguing seasonals. Phillips offers afternoon tours Wednesday thru Friday.

Though Victoria certainly has a higher concentration of breweries and brewpubs than other places on the island, there's great beer being made farther north (and on Salt Spring Island). Duncan has the Craig Street Brewpub, with its simple but well-rounded selection of offerings. Nanaimo is home to both the Longwood Brewpub, which has an ample selection of both English- and German-style brews, and the Fat Cat Brewery, which, in addition to its four regular offerings, does a bourbon-barrel-aged barley wine. The new kid on the block is Surgenor in Comox, which produces just three styles—lager, amber and pale ale—that are bottled and sold in six-packs. Salt Spring Island Ales takes advantage of that island's lovely mild climate to grow some of their own hops for their seasonal Golden Ale.

BREWPUBS

Canoe Brewpub, Marina and Restaurant
450 Swift Street, Victoria
T: 250-361-1940
W: canoebrewpub.com

Craig Street Brewpub

25 Craig Street, Duncan
T: 250-737-2337
W: craigstreet.ca

Longwood Brewpub

5775 Turner Road, Nanaimo
T: 250-729-8225
W: longwoodbrewpub.com

Spinnakers Gastro Brewpub

308 Catherine Street, Victoria
T: 250-386-2739
W: spinnakers.com

Swan's Brewpub and Buckerfields Brewery

506 Pandora Avenue, Victoria
T: 250-361-3310
W: swanshotel.com

CRAFT BREWERIES

Driftwood Brewing Company

102 – 450 Hillside Avenue, Victoria
T: 250-381-2739
W: driftwoodbeer.com

Fat Cat Brewery

2 – 940 Old Victoria Road, Nanaimo
T: 250-716-2739
W: fatcatbrewery.com

Lighthouse Brewing Company

2 – 836 Devonshire Road, Victoria

T: 250-383-6500

W: lighthousebrewing.com

Phillips Brewing Company

2010 Government Street, Victoria

T: 250-380-1912

W: phillipsbeer.com

Salt Spring Island Ales

270 Furness Road, Salt Spring Island

T: 250-653-2383

W: gulfislandsbrewery.com

Surgenor Brewing Company

861 Shamrock Place, Comox

T: 250-339-9947

W: surgenorbrewing.ca

Vancouver Island Brewery

2330 Government Street, Victoria

T: 250-361-0007

W: vanislandbrewery.com

EVENTS

The Great Canadian Beer Festival is held each year in Victoria on the first weekend after Labour Day with more than 50 craft breweries from across Canada, Belgium, and the US Pacific Northwest coming together to celebrate the diversity of the brewers' craft. For more information, visit gcbf.com.

SEASONAL RECIPES THAT PAIR WITH VANCOUVER ISLAND AND GULF ISLAND WINES

The Menu

A PERFECT MATCH:
CREATING A COASTAL CUISINE

Julie Pegg

Vancouver Island and Gulf Island wineries are springing up as quickly as you can pop a cork. As well, an influx of farmers, organic gardeners, bakers, and cheesemakers has made astonishing inroads into the region's culinary scene over the last few years. Innovative chefs, from white-linen restaurants to humble hole-in-the-walls, are seeking out their local farmers and fishers for the freshest produce, meats, and sustainable seafood. Many grow their own herbs and vegetables. Most have a good grip on local wine, or rely on the taste buds of the island's burgeoning number of sommeliers. What's more, our chefs are proud of like-minded wine folk who grow grapes on island soil. So there they are, proud to be plating and pouring year round. And here we are, presenting 16 recipes, from both established and emerging chefs, celebrating Vancouver Island's bounty.

We like that these dishes don't necessarily demand adherence to traditional food-and-wine-pairing tenets. The vibrant, aromatic, and often earthy notes predominant in island ingredients and wines allow for a little rule bending. Is it possible to match red wine with a fish recipe, or white wine with a lamb dish? We think it is.

Still, some basic, old-fashioned food-and-wine-pairing common sense applies, the key being that the dish and the wine never upstage each other. Pairings work best when body and flavour are in unison. Vancouver Island Pinot Gris, for example, ranges from austere and zesty to round and fleshy (but always with that zip of island acidity). While a lean wine would be ideal for oysters, a fatter version is a better match for halibut or oily sablefish. Ortega, the island's bread-and-butter varietal, hints at spicy apricot flavours—ideal for the similar-scented chanterelles that pop up in abundance at certain times of year. Bacchus and fruity, aromatic blends cozy up to island cheeses. So does the peppery red varietal

Zweigelt, due to its lack of grippy tannins. Earthy Pinot Noir with smoky morels? Perfect. And you will find the juiciest blackberries everywhere, both on the plate and in the glass.

The seasons govern island cuisine, and these recipes follow suit. Spring brings earthy morels and rapini atop thin strands of pasta with simple-roasted sablefish. We welcome summer with heirloom tomato gazpacho infused with roasted garlic and chipotle peppers, and celebrate the spot prawn's brief season with an aromatic Asian-style dish. It's impossible to segue into autumn without the chanterelle, so we offer duck breast with chanterelle orzo risotto (*orzotto*). Winter favours meaty lamb shanks, whose fragrant aromas fill the kitchen with cumin, coriander, and cloves. And spicy chai tea honey cake takes on all seasons, perhaps napped with rhubarb compote in spring, homemade peach ice cream in mid-summer or brandied cherries on frostier days. We also celebrate the abundant harvest with easy-to-make mead jelly, blackberry compote, pickled onions, and, our favourite, quince and apple butter.

These recipes will appeal to locals and visitors alike, from the everyday cook to the gourmet chef. If you are an out-of-towner, we hope these recipes inspire you to support your farmers and fishers. With a few tweaks and twists, you can adapt our recipes to your local flavours. Mostly, though, we wish to share with you the marvelous bounty of Vancouver Island. Enjoy.

Note: Recipes were tested in a domestic kitchen using market ingredients. Every stove is different and just as the same grape variety can vary in flavour depending on the soil, fresh ingredients can vary in characteristics depending on the garden, farm, or waters. Adjust cooking methods accordingly.

SPRING

Vegetable Ragout

8 baby golden beets
(do not substitute red beets)

Olive oil, for coating beets

6 medium-sized fingerling potatoes

Salt, for cooking water

12 thin to medium-thin asparagus spears

12 sugar snap peas

8 fresh morels (optional)

1 clove garlic, minced

¾ cup (185 mL) dry,
unoaked white wine

2 cups (500 mL) clear chicken stock
(homemade or a good-quality brand)

Halibut

4 5-oz (150 g) halibut
fillets, skin removed

Salt, for coating

3 Tbsp (45 mL) good-quality olive oil

Garnish

Coarse sea salt, to taste

Best-quality olive oil, to taste

Chopped chives (optional)

Braised Pacific Halibut with Spring Vegetable Ragout in a White Wine & Golden Beet Broth

This dish, blushing with a first kiss of spring, calls for a clean, crisp wine. Ortega's pure fruit notes partner well with the earthy sweetness of the beets and the succulent halibut, yet don't overwhelm the tender peas and asparagus. A fruity sparkling wine would fare equally well and truly celebrate the season's awakening.

Recommended wine: Ortega | Alternative: Sparkling wine

Preheat the oven to 400°F (200°C).

Rinse the beets, pat them dry, and rub lightly with olive oil. Wrap each beet in aluminum foil, place on a baking sheet (to catch any escaping juice), and roast until tender and pierced easily with a thin, sharp knife, about 1 hour. Cool, peel—skins should slip off easily when scraped with a knife—and then dice the beets. (Leave the oven on if you intend to finish the halibut fillets by baking.)

Halve the fingerling potatoes and place in a small saucepan. Cover with cold, salted water and bring to a boil. Simmer until tender, 3 to 5 minutes, then drain in a colander, dice, and set aside.

Snap the woody ends off the asparagus spears. Remove the strings from the snap peas. Prepare a bowl of ice water. On high heat, bring a pot of lightly salted water to a boil. Blanch each vegetable separately for about 20 to 30 seconds, and then transfer to the ice bath until cool.

If using, rinse the morels in 3 changes of cold water and pat dry.

Salt the halibut fillets lightly.

In an ovenproof sauté pan that is large enough to comfortably hold all 4 fillets, heat the olive oil on high to medium-high heat. When the oil is hot but NOT smoking, add the halibut and sear quickly on both sides, about 1 minute each side. Transfer the fillets to a plate.

Reduce the heat to medium. Add the beets and potatoes, then the asparagus and peas, morels (if using), and chopped garlic to the pan. Sauté for about 1 minute, or until the garlic is soft. Add the white wine and reduce the liquid by nearly half. Add the chicken stock and stir the mixture gently. Place the

halibut on top of the vegetables, cover the pan, and finish on top of the stove on low-medium heat, or, preferably, place the pan on the middle rack of a preheated 400°F (200°C) oven. Cook for 5 to 10 minutes. Be careful not to overcook the fish; the halibut should remain moist and flake easily with the nudge of a fork.

To serve, divide the vegetable ragout evenly among 4 shallow soup plates or pasta bowls. Add a fillet to each one and spoon 2 or 3 tablespoons (30 to 45 mL) of broth overtop. Sprinkle each dish with coarse sea salt to taste, and drizzle with your best-quality olive oil, and a few finely chopped chives if you like.

Editor's Tip: This dish demands the best-quality ingredients you can find. If asparagus or peas are unavailable, tender leeks sliced lengthwise sub in nicely. When preparing this dish outside of spring, look for the finest and freshest vegetables of the current season—for instance, use baby carrots and white turnips in late summer or fall.

Serves 4

Marinated Sablefish on Capellini with Rapini and Morels

Pinot Noir's earthy, somewhat tart fruit is a natural foil for the smoky morels and the bitter rapini, while cozying up to the rich, oily fish. Fruity Zweigelt offers similar characteristics but also lends a peppery zip to the dish.

Recommended wine: Pinot Noir | Alternative: Zweigelt

Fish

4 6 oz (175 g) sablefish fillets, skin left on

¼ cup (60 mL) Venturi-Schulze Brandenburg No. 3 wine (or substitute amontillado sherry)

Salt, for sprinkling prior to baking

Sauce

1.5 oz (45 g) dried morel mushrooms

4 Tbsp (60 mL) olive oil

1 medium shallot, thinly sliced

2 tsp (10 mL) minced garlic

1 cup (250 mL) reserved morel soaking liquid

½ cup (125 mL) chicken stock

¼ cup (60 mL) dry, unoaked white wine

10 stalks rapini (or substitute kale), chopped roughly

Salt and pepper, to taste

Pasta

¼ cup (125 mL) salt

½ lb (250 g) capellini (Capellini is a very thin variety of Italian pasta. Like spaghetti, it is rod-shaped, in the form of long strands, and thinner than vermicelli. It is available fresh or dried. We used dried for this recipe.)

Soften dried mushrooms by soaking in hot water for 20 minutes. Drain and set aside 1 cup (250 mL) of the soaking liquid.

In a shallow dish, marinate the fish in the wine for 1 hour, turning the fillets occasionally.

Place a 14-inch (35 cm) sauté pan on medium-high heat and add the olive oil. When the oil is hot, add the shallot and sauté till translucent, about 3 minutes. Turn down the heat to medium and add the garlic. Sauté the shallot and garlic for 1 minute. Add the morel liquid, chicken stock, and white wine; season to taste with salt and pepper. Turn the heat to high and reduce the liquid by half. Turn the heat to low and add the morels, and then the rapini. Toss the mushrooms and the greens well and continue to cook until the mushrooms are very tender and the greens are wilted, about 5 minutes. Remove from heat. Set sauce aside while you cook the fish and the pasta.

Preheat the oven to 475°F (240°C) and line a baking sheet with parchment paper. Remove the sablefish fillets from the marinade and pat very dry with paper towels. Place skin side down on the pan and sprinkle with salt.

Fill a stockpot with 10 cups (2.5 L) water and add the salt. Bring to a rolling boil on high heat. Add the capellini to the boiling water and cook according to package directions until al dente, about 6 minutes. When pasta is done, remove ¼ cup (60 mL) of the cooking water, then drain the pasta well.

Place the fillets in the preheated oven and cook for 6 to 8 minutes. Do not turn. Fish will flake easily when done and skin should be crispy. Sablefish can stand a fair amount of cooking before it dries out so don't worry if the pasta takes longer than 8 minutes to cook; keep the fish warm in the oven until needed.

Return the sauce to the stove on medium heat and add the capellini. Using tongs, toss the pasta and sauce, adding some of the reserved pasta water if the sauce is too thick.

To serve, use tongs to twirl a nest of pasta mixture into 4 shallow bowls. Top with any remaining sauce, and then add a piece of fish, skin side up. Drizzle with extra virgin olive oil.

Editor's Tip: If using fresh capellini, the cooking time will be about 3 minutes. Do not throw away any extra capellini; refrigerate it instead. Place it in a colander and pour boiling water overtop to reconstitute it. Serve with a simple sauce made from olive oil, white wine, garlic, olives, and a dash of chiles.

Serves 4

Spot Prawn "Pot au feu" in Coconut-Almond Broth

Coconut-Almond Broth

Shells from 20 spot prawns, prawns reserved for pot-au-feu

2 Tbsp (30 mL) kosher salt in a large bowl of cold water

1 tsp (5 mL) canola oil

1 medium shallot, peeled and sliced thin

5 whole coriander seeds, cracked with the flat side of a knife blade

¼ tsp (1 mL) whole black peppercorns, cracked with the flat side of a knife blade

¼ cup (60 mL) dry vermouth

2 fresh bay leaves (or good-quality dried bay leaves)

1 sprig fresh thyme

½ cup (125 mL) almond milk (preferably Almond Breeze or homemade)

1 quart (1 L) clear vegetable stock

1 10 oz (284 mL) can coconut milk, coconut cream reserved for pot-au-feu

Zest of 1 lime

Juice of 1 lime

A few leaves of cilantro

Pot-au-feu

4 baby turnips, quartered lengthwise and blanched

4 baby carrots, quartered lengthwise and blanched

1 celery heart, diced and blanched

20 whole blanched almonds

Coconut-almond broth

Coconut cream reserved from making broth

20 spot prawns, shelled, peeled, and blanched (thawed if necessary)

12 basil leaves

12 to 15 leaves of fresh cilantro

Innovative meets traditional in this Asian twist on traditional beef "pot-au-feu." Local spot prawns, coconut milk, and almond milk are matched with the dish's traditional vegetables: turnips, carrots, and celery. An off-dry sparkling wine sidles up to the sweetness of the prawns and broth, while the mineral nuance often found in a zippy Pinot Gris becomes good buddies with the vegetables' earthy notes.

Recommended wine: Sparkling wine | Alternative: Pinot Gris

Note: Coconut-Almond Broth can be made up to 2 days ahead and chilled until needed.

Preheat the oven to 200°F (90°C).

In a large, stainless steel bowl, rinse the prawn shells thoroughly in the salted water. Drain the shells and spread evenly on an ungreased baking sheet. Place in the oven and dry for 10 to 20 minutes. Using tongs, turn the shells intermittently until no water is visible on the tray or prawn shells. Remove the shells from the oven.

Heat the oil in a saucepan on medium-low heat. Add the prawn shells and sauté until the shells become aromatic and begin to turn pink. Add the shallot and spices. Continue to sauté until the shells are bright pink. (Be careful not to brown the bottom of the pot.) Deglaze with vermouth and add the bay leaves and herbs. Reduce until the shell mixture is almost dry, and then add the almond milk and stock. Reduce the mixture by two-thirds. Add the lime zest, coconut milk, and lime juice. Return to a simmer. Add the cilantro. Using a mesh sieve, strain the broth immediately into a bowl or lidded container, and set aside until the pot-au-feu is ready to assemble. Do not worry if the broth separates; it will come together when you add the coconut cream to the pot-au-feu.

Divide the vegetables and almonds among 4 warm bowls.

In a saucepan, reheat the coconut-almond broth on medium heat until hot but not boiling.

Adjust the seasoning, and then add the prawns. Cook for 15 seconds. With a slotted spoon, remove the prawns from the broth and place 5 in each bowl.

Add the coconut cream to the broth and, using a hand-blender, mix on high speed for 30 seconds until lightly foamy. Divide the hot broth immediately among the bowls and garnish with the herbs. Serve immediately.

Editor's Tips: To remove the shells from the prawns easily, blanch the prawns for 10 seconds and then plunge them into an ice bath. Remove the shells and reserve for stock, and place the prawns in a tub of salted ice water. Refrigerate or freeze the prawns and shells until needed.

To make your own almond milk, steep a good handful of roasted slivered almonds in ½ cup (125 mL) scalded milk. Refrigerate for 8 hours or overnight. Drain the milk from the almonds.

Work as quickly as possible when assembling the pot-au-feu in order to keep the broth hot and foamy, and to ensure prawns and vegetables remain crunchy.

If baby vegetables are not available, substitute small bunched carrots and small white turnips, sliced ¼ inch (6 mm) wide and 1½ inch (4 cm) long. Blanch as you would baby vegetables.

Leftover broth can be infused with rice to make a delicious congee.

Serves 4

Potatoes

1 lb (500 g) baby fingerling potatoes
(or substitute Yukon Gold nuggets)

Salt, for the boiling water

¼ cup (60 mL) unsalted butter

2 cloves garlic, crushed

2 Tbsp (30 mL) freshly
squeezed lemon juice

Zest of 1 lemon

Lavender Beurre Blanc

1 cup (250 mL) dry white wine

1 shallot, finely diced

1 Tbsp (15 mL) culinary
lavender flowers

¾ cup (185 mL) cold
unsalted butter, diced

Asparagus Salad

Bunch fat asparagus spears,
about 1 lb (500 g)

Small fennel bulb

½ cup (125 mL) shelled fresh peas

Small bunch flat-leaf Italian
parsley, roughly chopped

¼ cup (60 mL) freshly
squeezed lemon juice

Zest of 1 lemon

1 tsp (5 mL) honey, preferably fireweed

3 Tbsp (45 mL) extra virgin olive oil

Salt and pepper, to taste

Fish

Canola oil, for frying

4 trout, preferably from Sooke, about
12 to 16 oz (375 to 450 g) total, filleted

½ cup (125 mL) flour, measured onto
a large plate or baking dish and
seasoned with salt and pepper

Fresh lavender sprigs, for garnishing

Pan-seared Sooke Trout Fillets on Steamed Fingerling Potatoes with Lavender Beurre Blanc and Shaved Asparagus Salad

The scent and flavour of spring lavender, touch of honey, and strong hints of lemon beg for the crisp, floral notes of a vibrant Gewürztraminer with its roses-and-grapefruit flavour. Trout and Riesling are a traditional match. Ortega's fruity Riesling-like notes are well suited to the succulent trout and buttery potatoes.

Recommended wine: Gewürztraminer | Alternative: Ortega

Preheat the oven to 350°F (180°C).

Parboil the potatoes, skin on, in lightly salted water on high heat until tender-firm and a sharp knife pierces cleanly through them. Drain the potatoes. Place them in an ovenproof dish with the butter, garlic, lemon juice, and lemon zest. Cover the dish tightly with aluminum foil. Place the potatoes on the middle rack of the oven and bake until very tender, about 20 minutes. Reduce the temperature to 200°F (95°C) and keep the potatoes warm while you prepare the beurre blanc and the salad.

Put the wine, shallot, and lavender in a small saucepan and simmer for 2 to 3 minutes on low heat until the liquid is reduced by almost half. Strain the mixture through a fine sieve into a small metal mixing bowl. Add 1 cup (250 mL) water to the saucepan and bring it to a simmer on low heat. Set the mixing bowl on top of the saucepan. Whisk in the butter 1 cube at a time until it is emulsified. Keep warm on very low heat while you cook the fish.

Break off the tough asparagus ends. With a sharp vegetable peeler, use long smooth strokes to shave the asparagus into a large bowl. Remove the fennel fronds and stalks, and trim off any tough, brown outer bits of the bulb. Cut the bulb in half lengthwise. Slice thinly and then toss with the asparagus. Add the peas and parsley and toss all the ingredients gently. Refrigerate until ready to serve. (Make salad as close to serving as possible.)

Heat a cast-iron or heavy skillet on high heat until very hot. Add enough oil to cover the bottom of the pan with about ¼ inch (6 mm) and reduce the heat to medium-high. Dredge the trout evenly in the seasoned flour and then place slowly into the hot oil. Fry filleted trout skin side down until golden brown, about 5 minutes. (Be careful of sputters.) Flip the fish and brown the other side, about 3 minutes. Do not overcook. Fish is ready when it is opaque and flakes easily with a fork. **Note**: If your skillet cannot hold all the fish, fry 1 or 2 fillets at a time and keep warm in the oven with the potatoes.

Whisk together the lemon juice, lemon zest, honey, oil, salt, and pepper, and dress the salad lightly.

Divide the potatoes between 4 plates. On each plate, overlap 2 halves of filleted trout, skin side up, on top of the potatoes. Drizzle a generous spoonful of the lavender beurre blanc over the fish. Top with dressed asparagus salad and garnish with fresh sprigs of lavender.

Editor's Tip: It is easy to fillet a small trout. Remove the head with a thin, sharp knife. Holding the fish firmly, make an incision where you removed the head and run the knife through the flesh until you feel the bone. Run the knife through the fish and cleanly down the backbone until the top fillet separates from the rib cage. Remove and trim the fillet. Turn the fish over and, starting from the tail this time, run the knife up the rib cage to separate, and then trim, the second fillet. (Or you can get the fishmonger to do it.)

Also, make sure you source *edible* lavender flowers.

Serves 4

SUMMER

Chai Tea Honey Cake with Summer Fruits

Dry

1½ cups (375 mL) golden sugar

2½ cups (625 mL) flour

1 tsp (5 mL) salt

1 tsp (5 mL) baking powder

2 tsp (10 mL) baking soda

Wet

2 large eggs

1 large egg yolk

1¾ oz (22.5 mL) strong brewed black chai tea (Stash, Tazo, or homemade)

1 tsp (5 mL) vanilla extract

½ cup (125 mL) honey, preferably organic, unpasteurized fireweed honey

½ cup (125 mL) melted unsalted butter

½ cup (125 mL) buttermilk (or milk soured with a dash of vinegar), at room temperature

Although we refrain from mentioning specific wine pairings, the Brandenburg No. 3 is an exception because of its unique smoky oak and toffee notes, which play off the tea yet go so well with the cake's honey, ginger, and spice flavours. A blackberry dessert wine or a slightly sweet sparkler flatters the fresh or poached fruit (or fruit compote); pears, rhubarb, peaches, or, naturally, blackberries are perfect foils for this lovely, moist confection.

Recommended wine: Venturi-Schulze Brandenburg No. 3
Alternative: Sparkling wine, Blackberry dessert wine

Preheat the oven to 350°F.

In a large mixing bowl, sift (or mix well with a fork) the dry ingredients.

In a separate mixing bowl, beat well with a wooden spoon or whisk the wet ingredients.

Add the liquid mix to the dry mix and beat until smooth (the batter should be slightly thicker than pancake batter).

Pour the batter into a well-greased and lightly floured 9-inch × 12-inch (23 × 30 cm) cake pan.

Bake for 30 minutes or until the cake springs back to a light touch. A toothpick or the sharp tip of a knife should come out clean when inserted into the middle of the cake. Let cool before removing from the pan and slicing.

To serve, arrange the cake on a plate and serve with fresh fruit in season, cooked fruit, or a compote. (We also like it with toffee ice cream.)

Editor's Tip: The recipe does not work well if made with commercial honey. Also, use the recommended size of pan and make sure the batter is spread evenly, otherwise the cake will not set. This cake gets better over a couple of days, and will keep for a week or more in a cake tin (if you can make it last that long).

2 bulbs garlic

Olive oil, for rubbing on garlic

4 large ripe tomatoes, coarsely chopped

1 red pepper, seeded, white pith removed, and coarsely chopped

1 medium-sized cucumber, peeled, seeded, and diced

1 small red onion, coarsely chopped

1½ tsp (7.5 mL) smoked paprika

1 small dried chipotle pepper, softened in boiling water for about 10 minutes and drained

1½ tsp (7.5 mL) roasted cumin seeds

1½ tsp (7.5 mL) salt

1 tsp (5 mL) black pepper

1 tsp (5 mL) fresh thyme

Small handful of fresh basil leaves

Juice of 1 lemon

Juice of 1 lime

¼ cup (125 mL) dry white wine

⅓ cup (80 mL) olive oil

1 tsp (5 mL) Worcestershire sauce

24 oz (3 cups [750 mL]) tomato juice (optional)

The Masthead Restaurant
Roasted Garlic & Chipotle Gazpacho

This chilled gazpacho harmonizes Spain with Vancouver Island time by using heirloom tomatoes, organic garlic, and fresh basil. Such a refreshing dish begs for Ortega. The wine's suggested sweetness provides a suitable contrast to the tomato's acids while partnering with the sweet, soft roasted garlic. Or say *Olé* with a *rosado* (rosé). Though rosé hasn't quite the flavour interest, gazpacho and rosé are guaranteed to cool you down and perk you up on a hot August day.

Recommended wine: Ortega | Alternative: Rosé

Preheat the oven to 375°F (190°F). Trim off the tops of the garlic bulbs. Rub lightly with oil and wrap in aluminum foil. Roast for 45 minutes, or until the cloves are soft when pierced with the tip of a sharp knife. Squeeze the garlic from the cloves. Place all the ingredients, except the tomato juice (if using), in a blender and purée until the texture is between chunky and smooth. Chill for 2 to 4 hours. Add tomato juice, if needed, to reach desired consistency. Adjust seasonings to taste.

To serve, pour soup into chilled bowls and top with your choice of chopped caper berries, island chèvre, roasted hazelnuts, or tortilla chips, and maybe a couple of grilled spot prawns or Qualicum Bay scallops.

Editor's Tip: Using juicy heirloom tomatoes may negate the need to add tomato juice. Yellow and orange tomatoes make a marvelous gazpacho but are lower in acid. A few additional squeezes of lime will add some zip. For a milder, hotter, or smokier gazpacho, adjust the seasonings accordingly.

Serves 4 to 6

1 to 2 Tbsp (15 to 30 mL) safflower oil

4 oz (115 g) lean smoked bacon, thick-sliced and cut into ½ inch (1 cm) pieces

4 cloves garlic, minced

½ cup (125 mL) Pinot Gris (or dry white wine)

3 to 4 Tbsp (45 to 60 mL) unsalted butter

2 lb (1 kg) mussels, preferably from Salt Spring Island, rinsed thoroughly and debearded

Small bunch of basil, leaves only

Chile flakes to taste (optional)

Steamed Salt Spring Island Mussels with Pinot Gris, Garlic, Basil, and Cured Bacon

A Pinot Gris with a kiss of oak is well suited to butter and to the smoky notes of cured bacon that lace the winey broth. Fruit-driven Viognier zips together beautifully the basil and garlic (and the chili flakes, if using).

Recommended wine: Pinot Gris (preferably lightly oaked)
Alternative: Viognier

In a large sauté pan or cast-iron skillet, heat the oil on medium heat. Add the bacon and sauté until the bacon is cooked but not crisp, about 2 minutes. (Add a splash of water if the bacon starts to stick to the pan.) Add the garlic and cook, stirring occasionally, until soft but not brown, about another 2 minutes. Add the wine and whisk in the butter. Reduce the mixture slightly.

Increase the heat to high and add the mussels. Cover and cook, shaking the pan periodically, until the mussels open, about 5 minutes. (Discard any unopened mussels.)

With a slotted spoon, remove the mussels from the liquid and divide evenly among warmed shallow bowls. Remove the pan from the heat and stir in the basil. (Basil leaves should soften but not wilt.) Spoon broth over the mussels and serve immediately with garlic-rubbed crostini. Sprinkle a few chili flakes, if desired, over the mussel dish when serving.

Editor's Tip: Do not use dried basil. If fresh basil is not available, substitute Italian parsley or cilantro.

Serves 8 as a starter, or 4 as a main course

Lemon Thyme Baked Eggs with Wild Chanterelles on Toast

Baked Eggs

12 large eggs, preferably free-range, organic ones

¼ cup (60 mL) unsalted butter, at room temperature

1 cup (250 mL) whipping cream (35% M.F.)

¼ cup (60 mL) fresh lemon thyme leaves, divided

Sea salt, for sprinkling

Sautéed Mushrooms

1 lb (500 g) fresh chanterelles

2 Tbsp (30 mL) olive oil

2 oz (60 g) butter

1 clove garlic, crushed with the side of a large knife

1 tsp (5 mL) fresh thyme

Salt and pepper, to taste

6 thick slices rustic bread or brioche, grilled and spread with soft goat cheese

Both sparkling wine and Bacchus have enough perfumed fruit and citrus flavours to harmonize with the mushrooms' apricot notes and lemon-like thyme, as well as possessing the slight sweetness that eggs prefer in a wine. The wines' acidity, meanwhile, slices through the butter and cream.

Recommended wine: A slightly sweet sparkling wine
Alternative: Bacchus or an aromatic white blend

Prepare baked eggs by preheating the oven to 450°F (240°C). Butter 6 8-oz (250 mL) gratin dishes or ramekins and space evenly on a baking sheet.

In a heavy-bottomed saucepan, scald the cream on high heat. Add 2 tablespoons (30 mL) of the lemon thyme leaves. Remove from the heat, cover with a lid, and steep for 10 minutes. Strain the cream through a mesh sieve and discard the thyme leaves.

Pour about 2 tablespoons (30 mL) cream into each gratin dish, enough to cover the bottom. Crack 2 eggs into each dish, and sprinkle with the remaining 2 tablespoons (30 mL) lemon thyme leaves and a pinch of sea salt. Bake until the egg whites are set and yolks are still runny, about 10 to 15 minutes.

While the eggs are baking, prepare the sautéed mushrooms. Trim and clean the chanterelles with a soft brush (do not wash the mushrooms as they are very delicate). Tear large ones in half.

Heat the oil and butter in a large skillet until hot but not smoking. Add the garlic clove, thyme, and mushrooms. Season with salt and pepper and sauté the chanterelles on high heat. Cook until the mushrooms are golden brown and they have given up their liquid and almost all of it has cooked off.

Remove the pan from the heat, drain the mushrooms on paper towels, and set aside to keep warm. Remove and discard the garlic clove.

To serve, using tongs and a kitchen towel to protect your hands from burning, carefully transfer each gratin dish or ramekin to a luncheon plate covered with a cocktail napkin, doily, or sweet cicely leaf. Spread grilled bread or brioche with goat cheese and top with sautéed chanterelles. Serve immediately.

Editor's Tip: If fresh chanterelles are not available, substitute a mix of other wild mushrooms or criminis but keep in mind that you will miss out on the gorgeous fruity notes of chanterelles. In this case, a minerally Pinot Gris may be a better wine choice.

Serves 6

FALL

Duck Breasts

1 tsp (5 mL) ground anise (or substitute ground allspice)

1 Tbsp (15 mL) coarse salt

1 Tbsp (15 mL) cracked black peppercorns

1 to 2 Tbsp (15 to 30 mL) olive oil

4 boneless duck breasts

1 Tbsp (15 mL) butter

1 clove garlic

Orzo "Risotto"

2 Tbsp (30 mL) olive oil

1 small onion, minced

2 cloves garlic, minced

1 tsp (5 mL) chopped fresh thyme

1 cup (250 mL) orzo

2 to 3 cups (500 to 750 mL) chicken or mushroom stock

½ lb (250 g) fresh chanterelles (or substitute other wild mushrooms)

2 oz (60 g) goat cheese (chèvre)

Salt and pepper, to taste

Blackberry Jus

1 tsp (5 mL) olive oil

1 shallot, minced

1 cup (250 mL) fresh blackberries, plus more for garnishing

½ cup (125 mL) red wine

1 cup (250 mL) light beef broth, preferably homemade

2 Tbsp (30 mL) butter

Salt and pepper, to taste

Anise-spiced Crisp-skinned Duck Breast with Goat Cheese & Chanterelle Orzo "Risotto" and Blackberry Jus

Bordeaux-like Merlot's cherry-chocolate flavours suit the classic French influence of this dish to a "T." Alternately, the fleshy fruit associated with Marechal Foch and Foch blends showcase the spice-rubbed bird as well as the wild mushroom pasta. Cabernet Sauvignon, with its hallmark blackberry/blackcurrant flavours, is a natural match for the jus.

Recommended wine: Merlot

Alternative: Marechal Foch, a Foch blend, or Cabernet Sauvignon

Preheat the oven to 375°F (190°C).

In a small bowl, combine the anise, salt, and pepper. Rub over the duck breasts. Heat a large, ovenproof skillet on medium-high, and then add the olive oil. Heat the oil until it is hot but not smoking. Add the duck breasts, skin side down, and cook for 5 to 8 minutes, or until most of the fat is rendered and the skin is crisp. Using tongs, turn the duck breasts over and take the pan off the heat. Crush the clove of garlic using the side of a knife, leaving the skin intact. Add the garlic and the butter to the pan. Place the duck breasts in the oven for 5 to 8 minutes. (The flesh should remain a rosy pink). Remove from the oven and baste with the juices from pan. Wrap the duck breasts in aluminum foil and set aside while you prepare the "orzotto."

In a pot, bring the stock to a simmer on moderate heat. In a large saucepan, heat the olive oil on medium-high heat. Sauté the onion and garlic until soft, about 5 minutes. Add the thyme and the orzo, stirring well until the pasta is coated with oil. Use a ladle to transfer 1 cup (250 mL) stock to the saucepan, stirring until the liquid is nearly absorbed. Continue this process, stirring continually until nearly all the stock is used or the pasta is creamy and cooked al dente. Stir in the chanterelles and goat cheese. Stir the mixture gently, until the goat cheese has collapsed into the orzo and the mushrooms are cooked, about 5 to 8 minutes. Season to taste with salt, pepper, and additional fresh thyme.

In a saucepan, sauté the shallots until translucent. Add the blackberries and sauté until they begin to soften. Add the red wine and deglaze the pan. Reduce the berry/wine mixture to about 3 tablespoons (45 mL). Add the

broth and reduce again by three-quarters. Remove from heat and swirl in the butter. Strain through a mesh sieve. Season to taste with salt and pepper.

Divide and mound the risotto evenly. Slice the duck breasts diagonally and set atop the risotto. Nap the duck sparingly with blackberry jus. Garnish the plate with fresh blackberries.

Editor's Tip: Pork medallions and blueberries can be prepared in much the same way as the duck and blackberries. Sear ½-inch-thick (1 cm) pork medallions on both sides, keeping the meat slightly pink. Blueberries may require the addition of some blueberry juice, as they tend not to be quite a juicy as blackberries.

Serves 4

Artisanal Cheese & Country Ham Plate with Homemade Condiments

2 to 3 oz (60 to 90 g) assorted cheeses, preferably mild blue, Brie-style, and nutty island varieties

3 oz (90 g) Country ham

Selection of assorted condiments, preferably Quince and Apple Butter, Pickled Onions, Blackberry Compote, Mead Jelly (recipes follow)

(per person)

Contrary to popular belief, white wine pairs better with most cheeses than red wine does (excepting strong, crumbly cheddar or similar hard cheeses). Zippy, fruity Ortega cuts through the fat of the cheese while pairing with the sweet and savoury condiments. If red is the order of the day, Zweigelt's bright berry fruit, barely perceptible tannins, and peppery character work well, particularly with cheese and blackberry.

Recommended wine: Ortega | Alternative: Zweigelt

Set out cheeses and ham attractively on a cheese board, or large square plate.

Place condiments in small ramekins or pots, along with small spoons and a tiny fork for spearing onions.

Editor's Tip: Add pork pâté and sausage for a red wine-friendly charcuterie plate.

Quince and Apple Butter

Yields 8 to 10 cups (2 to 2.5 L)

8 apples
8 quinces
2 cinnamon sticks
1 bay leaf
5 star anise
1½ tbsp (22.5 mL) fresh rosemary sprigs
1 cup (250 mL) sugar

Peel and quarter the apples and quince and combine the pieces in a large pot containing 4 cups (1 L) water. Bring to a boil on high heat. Cook, stirring constantly, until the fruit is completely falling apart.

Pass the fruit through a food mill on the smallest setting, or press through a fine mesh sieve, reserving the water used to boil the fruit. Return this water to the pot along with the strained fruit.

Tie the cinnamon, bay leaf, star anise, and rosemary in a piece of cheesecloth and add to the pot.

Slowly stir in the sugar. Bring to a boil and cook until the mixture thickens and begins to sputter, about 7 minutes. Cool, and then put into preserving jars.

Refrigerate in an airtight container for up to 2 months, or process jars in a boiling-water canner according to the manufacturer's directions.

9 cups (2.25 L) white vinegar
5 cups (1.25 L) white sugar
1 cup (250 mL) water
¾ cup (185 mL) kosher salt
3 large onions, sliced thinly

Pickled Onions

This recipe may also be used for pickling beets, green beans, carrots, or cauliflower.

Yields 1 quart (1 L)

Combine the vinegar, sugar, water, and salt in a large saucepan and bring to a boil on high heat. Boil rapidly for 1 minute, and then remove the pickling brine from the heat.

Place the onions in a 1-quart (1 L) mason jar and cover with pickling brine. Let sit in the refrigerator for 24 hours. If not using immediately, process and seal in a boiling-water canner according to the manufacturer's directions. Store for at least 3 weeks in a cool, dry place before serving.

Blackberry Compote

Yields 6 cups (1.5 L)

10 cups (2.5 L) fresh blackberries
5 cups (1.25 L) white sugar
4 Tbsp (60 mL) crushed juniper berries
1 bay leaf
1 tsp (5 mL) ground black pepper
1 package pectin (optional)

Crush the blackberries using a potato masher and add to a large saucepan. Bring to a boil on high heat, and then add the sugar, juniper berries, bay leaf, and black pepper. Stir in the pectin, if using, and return to a boil for 1 minute. Continue stirring for 5 minutes. Pour cooled compote into preserving jars. Store for 3 weeks before using.

Mead Jelly

Yields 2 cups (500 mL)

2 cups (500 mL) mead, preferably from Vancouver Island
1 cup (250 mL) sugar
1 sprig fresh rosemary

1 pouch unflavoured gelatin
½ cup (125 mL) boiling water, divided

In a large saucepan, bring the mead to a boil. Stir in the sugar and rosemary.

Pour ¼ cup (125 mL) boiling water into a bowl, and then add the gelatin. Pour the remaining ¼ cup (125 mL) water overtop and stir until the gelatin is fully dissolved. Pour through a strainer into the sweetened mead.

Transfer the liquid to a 16-ounce (500 mL) jelly or preserving jar, remove the sprig of rosemary, and let sit overnight.

Refrigerate for up to 1 month, or process the jar in a boiling-water canner according to the manufacturer's directions.

Chamomile-Lavender Tea Scented Scallops with Jerusalem Artichoke Purée and a Tea & Verjus Reduction

Scallops

1 Tbsp (15 mL) loose-leaf chamomile-lavender tea (or substitute Earl Grey)

2 tsp (10 mL) loose-leaf black tea, such as Darjeeling

½ cup (125 mL) boiling water

¼ cup (60 mL) verjus (or substitute crisp white wine)

Zest from 1 lemon

Juice from 2 lemons

2 tsp (10 mL) fresh thyme leaves

2 Tbsp olive oil, divided

12 bay scallops, preferably from Qualicum Bay

Salt and pepper, for seasoning

2 Tbsp (30 mL) butter

Jerusalem Artichoke Purée

1 lb (500 g) Jerusalem artichokes (also known as sunchokes), peeled

1½ cups (325 mL) table cream (18% M.F.)

Salt and pepper, to taste

2 Tbsp (30 mL) butter

Fried sage leaves or chopped chives, for garnishing

The succulence of these luscious, perfumed scallops combines with the creamy Jerusalem artichoke purée to create a perfect pairing for a wine brimming with honeysuckle and orange or pear-blossom aromatics. Riesling's relative, Bacchus, or a perfumey Schonburger, Siegerrebe, Madeleine Sylvaner, or a blend made from these varietals, would perfectly showcase this dish.

Note: Verjus is the acidic juice made from pressing unripe grapes.

Recommended wine: Bacchus

Alternative: Another aromatic white or white blend

In a blender, whirl the tea, boiling water, verjus, lemon zest, lemon juice, and thyme and 1 tablespoon (15 mL) olive oil until well emulsified.

Place the scallops in a stainless steel mixing bowl and pour the marinade overtop. Mix well to coat. Cover the bowl with plastic wrap and refrigerate for 60 to 90 minutes, making sure the marinade does not "cook" the scallops. (Scallops should remain opalescent and springy to the touch.)

While the scallops are marinating, prepare the Jerusalem artichoke purée. Place the Jerusalem artichokes in a medium-sized saucepan. Add the cream and just enough water to barely cover them. Scald the cream, and then lower the heat and simmer the Jerusalem artichokes in the cream until they are tender, about 15 to 20 minutes. Using a slotted spoon, transfer them to a food mill or food processor. Slowly add enough liquid from the saucepan and purée until the Jerusalem artichokes become creamy and smooth. Set aside, and heat through gently just prior to serving.

With a slotted spoon, transfer the marinated scallops to paper towels and pat dry. Reserve the marinade by straining it into a non-reactive bowl. Season the scallops with salt and pepper.

Heat the remaining 1 tablespoon (15 mL) olive oil in a skillet on high heat. Using tongs, sear the scallops on all sides until caramelized and just barely cooked through, about 3 minutes. Transfer the cooked scallops to a plate and let them rest in a warm place.

Deglaze the pan with the reserved marinade and cook until reduced to ½ cup (125 mL). Remove from the heat and whisk in the butter until well combined.

To serve, divide the warm Jerusalem artichoke purée among 4 plates. Place 3 scallops atop each mound of purée and drizzle with sauce. Garnish with fried sage leaves or fresh chopped chives. Serve with sautéed Swiss chard or baby spinach.

Editor's Tip: Some scallops contain more moisture than others so adding a little more verjus or wine to the reserved marinade may be necessary to make the sauce.

Serves 4

Crab Filling

1 lb (500 g) fresh Dungeness crabmeat

½ lb (250 g) Brie, slightly softened, rind removed and sliced thin

Zest of 1 lemon

Zest of 1 lime

Zest of 1 orange

1 Tbsp (15 mL) juice from the lemon, lime, and orange

2 cloves garlic, minced

3 green onions, sliced

Roasted Peppers & Onions

2 red peppers, halved, seeded, and sliced ½ inch (1 cm) wide

½ red onion, sliced into rings about ¼ inch (0.5 cm) thick

1 Tbsp (15 mL) freshly squeezed lemon juice

Olive oil, for coating

Tomato-Corn Salsa

6 Roma tomatoes, seeded and chopped

1 cup (250 mL) corn kernels (preferably from 2 ears fresh corn boiled for 10 minutes)

1 medium-sized Spanish onion, finely chopped

2 cloves garlic, minced

Juice of 1 lime

2 to 4 Tbsp (30 to 60 mL) olive oil

1 tsp (5 mL) roasted cumin seeds

Salt and pepper, to taste

Lime Crème Fraîche

¾ cup (185 mL) crème fraîche (or substitute sour cream)

Zest of 1 lime

1 Tbsp (15 mL) freshly squeezed lime juice

6 10-inch (25 cm) flour tortillas

1 to 2 tsp (5 to 10 mL) grapeseed or canola oil, for frying

Aura Waterfront Restaurant & Patio

Dungeness Crab & Brie Quesadillas with Roasted Peppers & Onions, Tomato-Corn Salsa and Lime Crème Fraîche

The sweet nature of corn and Dungeness crab are made for buttery Chardonnay. Vancouver Island grows little Chardonnay but a similarly rich, fat white wine buoyed by good acid, such as an oaked Pinot Gris or a full-bodied Ortega, will have enough body and weight to stand up to the corn and crab, as well as complement the Brie's creamy texture.

Note: The salsa is best made a day or two ahead of time.

Recommended wine: Oaked Pinot Gris | Alternative: Ortega

Combine crab filling ingredients and mix well. Cover and refrigerate.

Toss the red pepper slices and onion rings in lemon juice and enough olive oil to coat. Place on an ungreased baking sheet and roast for 5 to 10 minutes, or until the vegetables are tender and beginning to brown. Cool, and then refrigerate.

Combine the salsa ingredients. Cover and refrigerate.

Stir the lime juice and lime zest into the crème fraîche (or sour cream). Cover and refrigerate.

Place 6 tortillas on your working surface. Divide the crab mix into 6 equal portions and spread evenly over one half of each tortilla. Top with roasted peppers and onions. Fold the tortilla in half to make a semicircle. (Quesadillas may be refrigerated at this point until you're ready to fry them.)

Preheat the oven to 200°F (90°C). Heat a large, non-stick skillet on medium-high. Add 1 to 2 teaspoons (5 to 10 mL) oil to the pan. (You will need 1 to 2 teaspoons of oil for each quesadilla.) Brown each quesadilla, about 2 minutes per side, and then transfer to a large baking sheet in the oven to keep warm.

When you have browned the last quesadilla, remove the others from the oven and cut each one in half. Place 2 halves, overlapping slightly, on each plate. Add a generous spoonful of salsa to the side and top with a dollop of crème fraîche.

Editor's Tip: If crab is unavailable, fresh shrimp are a good substitute.

To make your own crème fraîche, mix 1 cup (250 mL) heavy whipping cream (35% M.F.) with 2 Tbsp (30 mL) buttermilk in a non-reactive bowl. Cover with plastic wrap and set in a warm, draft-free place overnight. Once thickened, refrigerate until needed.

Serves 6

WINTER

Braised Indian-style Lamb Shanks with Cumin-Mint Raita

Spice Rub

1 Tbsp (15 mL) ground black pepper

2 tsp (10 mL) coarse salt

2 tsp (10 mL) ground coriander

2 tsp (10 mL) ground cumin

2 tsp (10 mL) ground cloves

2 to 3 tsp (10 to 15 mL) grapeseed oil (optional)

Lamb Shanks

4 to 6 meaty lamb shanks

¼ to ½ cup (60 to 125 mL) vegetable oil

1 medium carrot, coarsely chopped

1 medium onion, coarsely chopped

4 cloves garlic, peeled

½ cup (125 mL) fresh ginger, coarsely chopped

2 ripe tomatoes, coarsely chopped

½ orange, rind removed and diced

½ lime, rind removed and diced

2 Tbsp (30 mL) mild curry paste

½ Tbsp (7.5 mL) tamarind paste (or substitute 1 Tbsp [15 mL] Worcestershire sauce)

2 cups (500 mL) beef stock

2 cups (500 mL) red wine or water

½ bunch cilantro, finely chopped

Cumin-Mint Raita

½ medium-sized cucumber, seeded

1 cup (250 mL) plain whole-milk yogurt

1 tsp (5 mL) ground cumin

2 Tbsp (30 mL) fresh mint, coarsely chopped

1 tsp (5 mL) honey

Salt and white pepper, to taste

Hardy Marechal Foch has a deep, dark intensity that stands up to this dish's exotic fruit-and-spice richness. But a Merlot with a bit of age and good acid would also fare well and heighten the complexity of the dish.

Recommended wine: Marechal Foch or a Foch blend | Alternative: Merlot

Preheat the oven to 350°F (180°C).

In a mixing bowl, combine the spice rub ingredients with a smidgen of oil to bind together the spices.

Rub shanks generously with spice mixture. In a Dutch oven or deep casserole dish with lid, brown shanks in batches about 5-8 minutes. Keep them from touching, otherwise shanks will not brown. Using tongs transfer shanks to a bowl.

In the same pan, add the carrot, onion, garlic, and ginger and sauté until tender, and they begin to take on colour, about 8 minutes. Whisk in the tomatoes, citrus fruit, curry paste, and tamarind paste. Return the shanks to the pan, and add enough stock and wine to cover the shanks. Bring the shanks to a simmer on medium heat, and then cover. (If the pan does not have a lid, cover it with aluminum foil.) Simmer for about 10 minutes.

Return the pan to the oven and immediately reduce the heat to 325°F (160°C). Cook for 2½ to 3 hours, or until the lamb nearly falls from the bone. After about 75 minutes, add the chopped cilantro. Check from time to time to see if any liquid has evaporated, adding more stock, wine, or water as needed.

Remove the lamb shanks from the oven and lift them out of the braising liquid, which should now have the consistency of gravy. Set the lamb shanks aside in a large dish and cover with foil. Keep warm.

Prepare the sauce for serving by removing the chopped ginger from the "gravy" with a slotted spoon and then purée the sauce. Set aside and keep warm while you prepare the raita.

Grate the cucumber onto a clean dishtowel or into a fine, mesh colander. Squeeze the towel tightly, or press hard on the grated cucumber, to remove any water. Combine the cucumber with the remaining ingredients and mix well.

To serve, place lamb shanks on serving plates. Spoon sauce overtop and dollop with raita. Serve with grilled flatbread or naan.

Editor's Tip: Grind whole spices in a coffee or spice grinder for the best flavour. Shanks are best made 1 day ahead. Refrigerate and remove the top layer of fat before reheating and serving.

Serves 4 to 6

Bison Tournedos

6 4 oz (175 g) bison tenderloins

1 tsp (5 mL) each of dried rosemary, thyme, sea salt, and crushed peppercorns mixed with enough olive oil to combine

6 rashers of double-smoked streaky bacon

Braised French Lentils

⅓ cup (80 mL) diced onion

1 small stalk celery with leaves, chopped

1 Tbsp (15 mL) butter

1 cup (250 mL) Puy lentils

2 cups (500 mL) chicken stock

1 bay leaf

1 Tbsp (15 mL) each of fresh sage, fresh thyme, and fresh rosemary, all finely chopped

Handful of Italian parsley, finely chopped

Salt and pepper, to taste

Garnish

6 cippolini onions (or large shallots) caramelized in 2 Tbsp (30 mL) olive oil, warm

2 Tbsp (30 mL) lavender jelly (or substitute another herb jelly)

¾ cup (185 mL) Brown Sauce (recipe on page 196), warm

Grilled Island Bison Tournedos with Double-Smoked Bacon, Lavender Jelly, and Braised French Lentils

This rich and lovely bison-tenderloin dish draws from classic French cooking methods and demands an equally opulent wine. A blend of Marechal Foch, Cabernet, and Merlot has the complexity to stand up to the bison, bacon, and sauce, and enough aromatics to complement the dish, while Pinot Noir flatters the ancillary flavours of the ragout, bacon, onions, and lavender jelly. Hint: to ensure game stays tender when cooked, add a little red wine and soy sauce to the spice and herb rub. Refrigerate tournedos for a few hours to relax the meat's fibre.

Recommended wine: Marechal Foch or a blend of Marechal Foch, Cabernet, and Merlot | Alternative: An earthy, full-bodied Pinot Noir

Preheat the oven to 300°F (150°C).

In an ovenproof braising pan or saucepan, sweat the onion and celery in the butter on low heat until translucent. Add the lentils and sauté with the vegetables for about 5 minutes. Add the chicken stock, bay leaf, and fresh herbs.

Bring the mixture to a boil and reduce to a simmer. Remove the pan from the heat and place in the oven. Braise for 30 to 40 minutes; the lentils should be tender but still firm.

While the lentils are cooking, preheat the barbecue to medium heat. (If using a charcoal grill, make sure coals are ash-grey.)

Rub the bison tenderloins all over with the herb and spice mixture, and then wrap in bacon. Secure bacon to each steak with a toothpick.

Place tournedos on the grill and cook until medium rare, about 4 to 6 minutes per side. Do not overcook or the meat may become tough and dry.

Divide braised lentils among 6 plates, about 4 tablespoons (60 mL) per plate, and gently top with a tournedo. Add a caramelized onion and nap with a teaspoon (5 mL) of lavender jelly. Drizzle brown sauce overtop each tournedo and around the lentils.

Editor's Tip: Purchased veal or beef stock works well for this dish. Better still, choose a rainy day, put on your best Julia Child imitation, and make a quantity of brown stock and brown sauce. Warm beefy aromas will fill the kitchen and a velvety, luxuriant sauce will reward your efforts. Keep brown sauce on hand for the bison recipe, but also for Madeira, mushroom, or peppercorn sauces, and to flavour stews and soups.

The braised lentils can also be made well ahead. When reheating, add a little stock to prevent them from becoming dry.

Serves 6

Brown Stock

3 to 4 lb (1.5 to 1.8 kg) meaty beef bones
2 large carrots, peeled and diced
2 large yellow onions, peeled and diced
2 celery stalks with leaves, diced
1 to 2 bay leaves
1 tsp (5 mL) dried thyme or a few fresh sprigs
1 tsp (5 mL) black peppercorns, crushed
2 cloves garlic, peeled and crushed
2 Tbsp (30 mL) tomato paste

Yields about 3 quarts (3 L)

Preheat the oven to 400°F (200°C).

In a shallow roasting pan, or a large cake pan, arrange the bones in a single layer. Roast the bones for 40 to 45 minutes, turning them occasionally so that they brown evenly. Remove the bones and place in an ovenproof stockpot. Pour the fat from the roasting pan into a heat-proof measuring cup and set it aside. Lower the oven heat to 350°F (180°C).

Place the roasting pan on medium-high heat on top of the stove. Deglaze the pan with ¼ to ½ cup (60 to 125 mL) cold water and then add the deglazing liquid to the stockpot. Return 2 tablespoons (30 mL) of the reserved beef fat to the roasting pan. (Be careful as the fat may spit).

On medium-high heat, sauté the vegetables in the roasting pan until they start to caramelize, about 8 minutes. Add the vegetables to the stockpot, along with enough water to cover the bones. Add the bay leaf, herbs, seasoning, and tomato paste.

On high heat, bring the stock to a boil, and then reduce to a simmer. Return the stockpot to the oven and cook for about 3 to 4 hours, or until the meat falls away easily from the bones when nudged with a fork. Check the pot occasionally to make sure the stock is not evaporating, topping up with water as necessary.

Remove the stock from the oven, and strain the liquid into a heat-proof bowl. Cool and refrigerate. When the stock is thoroughly cooled, skim off any congealed beef fat, and refrigerate or freeze stock.

Brown Sauce (adapted from Julia Child)

3 Tbsp (45 mL) butter or cooking oil
¼ cup (60 mL) each of carrots, onions, and celery leaves
3 Tbsp (35 mL) lean bacon, finely diced (or fatty bacon simmered in water for 10 minutes, drained, and then diced)
1½ Tbsp (22.5 mL) flour
4 cups (1 L) Brown Stock, preferably homemade
1 Tbsp (15 mL) tomato paste
1 bay leaf
1 tsp (5 mL) dried thyme
4 sprigs parsley
1 tsp (5 mL) cracked peppercorns

Yields 1 quart (1 L) (Recipe can also be doubled or quadrupled for freezing)

In a stockpot on medium-low to medium heat, sauté the vegetables and bacon in butter or oil for about 10 minutes.

Blend the flour slowly into the vegetables and stir continually until the flour is nut brown, about another 8 to 10 minutes. Remove from the heat and whisk in the brown stock and tomato paste. Add the herbs and reduce the heat to low.

Simmer for about 2 hours, skimming the foam that forms off the top from time to time. When the sauce is ready, it should lightly coat the back of a spoon. Strain the sauce into a bowl, pressing the stock from the solids.

Cool, refrigerate, and degrease. Sauce is ready to use, or can be stored in the refrigerator or freezer.

Garlic & Parsley Compound Butter

½ cup (125 mL) unsalted butter, softened

1 tsp (5 mL) minced garlic

2 Tbsp (30 mL) minced shallot

½ cup (125 mL) finely chopped fresh flat-leaf parsley

2 Tbsp (30 mL) freshly squeezed lemon juice

Pinch of salt

Ground black pepper, to taste

Oysters

½ cup (125 mL) Ortega or Pinot Gris

6 medium-sized to large oysters, shucked, 6 half shells reserved and scrubbed clean

Coarse salt or aluminum foil

Freshly grated Parmigiano-Reggiano cheese

Baked Quadra Island Oysters with Garlic & Parsley Compound Butter

These pearls of the ocean plucked right from island shores bathe gently in white wine, and then are baked and broiled ever so briefly beneath a light Parmigiano-Reggiano crust. The clean minerality of Pinot Gris loves the oysters' brininess, while the added weight of an Ortega tackles the butter and cheese. And who can resist serving classic bubbly with these briny molluscs for a romantic evening?

Recommended wine: Pinot Gris | Alternative: Ortega or a sparkling wine

In a food processor, or using a bowl and a wooden spoon, blend the butter, shallots, chopped parsley, lemon juice, salt, and pepper until creamy. Refrigerate while you prepare the oysters.

Preheat the oven to 400°F (200°C).

Cover an 8-inch (20 cm) square baking pan with coarse salt or crumpled aluminum foil to anchor the oysters during baking.

In a 10-inch (25 cm) sauté pan, bring the wine slowly to a gentle simmer. Slide the oysters gently into the wine, and then remove the pan from the heat. Let the oysters "bathe" for 1 minute. With a slotted spoon, lift the oysters carefully from the poaching liquid and place each one in a cleaned half shell. Place the oysters on the salt bed or the bunched aluminum foil.

Dot each oyster with a generous teaspoon (5 mL) of compound butter.

Bake the oysters until the butter is completely melted and the oysters are barely cooked, about 10 minutes. Remove from the oven and scatter a teaspoon (5 mL) or so of grated cheese overtop each one.

Turn the oven's temperature to broil and return the oysters to the top shelf. Watching all the time, broil the oysters until the cheese topping starts to turn golden brown, about 1 to 3 minutes.

To serve, place each oyster on a small doily-covered plate.

Editor's Tip: Allow 2 oysters per person. Serve with a side salad of island micro-greens simply dressed with verjus and a touch of walnut or hazelnut oil. Finish with a tayberry sorbet for a lovely light luncheon.

Allow 2 oysters per person or double the recipe to serve 6.

Paprika Chicken Livers

1 cup (250 mL) duck or chicken fat (or substitute lard)

1 medium onion, finely diced

1 green pepper, seeded and quartered

1 clove garlic, smashed with a little oil and coarse salt

1 lb (500 g) chicken livers, preferably from free-range chickens, rinsed and patted dry

1 Tbsp (15 mL) good-quality paprika

¾ tsp (4 mL) kosher salt

Basketful toasted or grilled crusty bread, for serving

The mellow, rich flavours of the chicken livers love the texture and taste of opulent fruit in either red or white wine. Fruity Pinot Noir or Merlot is a friendly match for the livers while the riper, richer style of Ortega or apple-like flavour of Bacchus works wonderfully with the paprika.

Recommended wine: Pinot Noir or Merlot | Alternative: Ortega or Bacchus

In a 10-inch (25 cm) skillet, heat the duck or chicken fat on medium heat until it melts. Add the onion, green pepper, and garlic clove. Sauté until the onion begins to take on colour, about 6 to 8 minutes. With a slotted spoon, remove the onion, pepper, and bits of garlic; discard them.

Leave the remaining fat in the skillet and return to medium heat before adding the livers (halved first if large-ish). Cook until barely firm, about 6 to 8 minutes. Add the paprika and the salt. Stir and let cool.

Using a fine mesh strainer, separate the livers from the fat. Divide the chicken livers evenly among the ramekins and pour the remaining fat and juice overtop. Refrigerate overnight before serving. (Chicken livers can be wrapped in plastic and refrigerated for up to 1 week, or frozen for up to 2 months.)

To serve, bring the chicken livers to room temperature, and spread on toasted or grilled rustic bread.

Editor's Tip: The discarded onions and peppers are delicious stirred into scrambled eggs.

Duck (or chicken) fat is far superior to lard in this recipe. Duck fat and lard are available for purchase at Stage.

Serves 6

Getting there is half the fun: between winery visits stop for plenty of breaks at local farms, cafés and restaurants.

TOURING THE WINE REGION

Kathryn McAree

If you love to eat and drink, and you enjoy seeking out new spots to indulge in discovering the people behind the passion, then you are a culinary tourist. Visiting the wineries of Vancouver Island and the Gulf Islands will be a welcome addition to any pleasure-seeking weekend or getaway. The following information is meant to provide you with ideas for the perfect culinary tour, from a culinary-tour operator and radio host who does more than her share of eating and drinking.

What I love best about the boutique and farm-gate wineries of the islands is the comfortable feel when you drop in. Spring, summer, or fall, there are always whites and reds to sip and sometimes a fruity dessert wine, often fortified, made from the vast quantities of blackberries that grow wild just about everywhere.

There are also numerous spots to visit and taste away in addition to wineries, cideries, and distilleries. The cheeseries, bakeries, markets, and restaurants along the way are quaint and convivial. Just make sure you plan your outing in advance and be prepared to indulge!

COWICHAN VALLEY

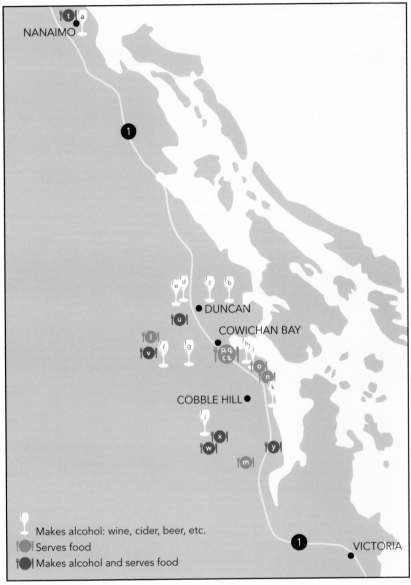

Makes alcohol: wine, cider, beer, etc.

Serves food

Makes alcohol and serves food

NANAIMO

DUNCAN

COWICHAN BAY

COBBLE HILL

VICTORIA

COWICHAN VALLEY

The Cowichan Valley has been referred to as the "Provence of North America" by many, most notably by the late James Barber, a Cowichan resident in his later years. Cookbook author, chef, and TV host best known as "The Urban Peasant," Barber visited the old fishing village of Cowichan Bay daily, enjoying favourite spots like True Grain Bread and Hilary's Cheese & Deli. It is a perfect place to begin your tour of the Cowichan Valley.

From Victoria, drive north up the picturesque Malahat. When locals say "the Malahat," we are referring to Highway 1, which is on the mountain called—you guessed it—the Malahat. Though this stretch of road can be treacherous in the winter if snow hits at the higher elevations, in the spring, summer, and fall, it is a gorgeous drive. If you happen to be touring in the fall, be sure to stop to see the salmon run in Goldstream Provincial Park just north of Victoria. You'll know your timing is right if you see cars parked along the side of the highway as the city road turns into the Malahat Drive.

Driving from downtown Victoria, you can be in Cowichan Bay Village in just an hour. Turn right on Cowichan Bay Road off Highway 1 and follow the road as it weaves its way down to the village of Cowichan Bay. Then follow your nose to True Grain Bread where they mill their own flour. See the mill and sample from their array of baked goods with a cup of organic coffee. My favourite is the chocolate buns, a white bread dough studded with organic, dark Callebaut chocolate. Apple strudel and traditional German pretzels are also hits but True Grain is really known for its many varieties of bread, baked fresh each day with various flours, including emmer, spelt, kamut, and Red Fife wheat, Canada's original wheat, which is being brought back by the purists. On Saturdays, they even have a loaf made with Red Fife wheat grown within five kilometres at a nearby farm. It doesn't get more local than that.

Now that you've covered a little breakfast, pop in next door to Hilary's Cheese & Deli. You are sure to be overwhelmed by the marvellous aroma of homemade soup simmering on the stove; it's made fresh each day. Hilary's is also a great spot for lunch or to pick up picnic supplies, including their local cow- and goat-milk cheeses.

Hilary and Patty Abbott have been making cheese in "the valley" for years. Their farm is on Cherry Point Road, along with the cheesemaking facility. Their soft goat cheese is rich and creamy and always in demand. Brie- and Camembert-style cheeses, both goat and cow, are great smothered on True Grain Bread's French baguettes. If you prefer your cheese a bit firmer, the Red Dawn and Belle Ann are tomme-style cheeses, rind-washed with Cowichan Blackberry, a port-like wine from Cherry Point Estate Wines. Or go for the gusto and try the blue cheeses. All are full-flavoured and divine!

Step out from Hilary's shop and stroll the docks and through the marina. Take a peek around the rest of the village and, if you've stayed too long, return to the café overlooking the water at Hilary's and have that soup you immediately smelled when you walked in the door. My favourite is the coconut Thai chicken soup accompanied by a French baguette sandwich made fresh each day with bread from True Grain Bread next door. You can mingle with the locals and relax in the quaint café.

The best part about lunching in "the bay" is that you will need dessert. Udder Guy's is just a few steps away, with locally made ice cream in a whole host of flavours. Since there is an eventual wine theme to the day, try the red wine grape ice cream or, a Cowichan favourite, wild blackberry. This is the cherry on top of a visit to Cowichan Bay Village.

Depart the bay the way you came: up Cowichan Bay Road. A short distance from the bay you will see Cowichan Bay Farm on the righthand side. Turn in slowly and make your way up the drive and past the home of Cowichan farmers Lyle and Fiona Young. This fourth-generation farm is beautifully preserved, thanks to the great work of the Young family and Lyle's grandfather. Park near the shop that bears the old "Sausages" sign and take a peek inside. This self-serve shop is indicative of the Cowichan community—welcoming and generous. Help yourself to fresh poultry from the walk-in fridge or chicken sausages, livers, or duck confit

The great outdoors, a picnic, and a bottle of wine . . . what more do you need?

from the freezer. Write your own receipt and drop it in the box along with your payment. I love it.

After touring and eating, it's certainly got to be an acceptable hour to start sipping wine.

There are several wineries to choose from, and this suggested route will keep you on track without the necessity of U-turns on the highway. There are other wineries as well, but too many to see in just one day.

Take the first right past Cowichan Bay Farm onto Koksilah Road. Follow it to Parker Road and turn left. (If you hit the highway, you've gone too far.) Follow this road, staying to the right when Parker Road runs to the left, and you will be on Myhrest Road where you will see Rocky Creek Winery on your right. There is a down-home feeling at this family-run winery where you are able to stroll through their backyard into the tiny tasting room. One of the owners, Mark or Linda, is bound to be there to greet you; they are always happy to share their stories. You will finish your tasting with their blackberry dessert wine and a bit of salted chocolate. This is a delicious combination.

Back out to Koksilah Road, turn right and follow it across Cowichan Bay Road and all the way to the end. You're taking a somewhat less direct route to Cherry Point Estate Wines, but it's a beautiful drive. When you reach the end of Koksilah

Road there is a stop sign. Turn right onto Cherry Point Road. Notice the first farm on the right, which is the home and production facility of Hilary's Cheese. Honk and wave as you go by!

This stretch of Cherry Point Road is one of my favourites in the Cowichan Valley. There's no particular reason, except for the fact that it's a bucolic heaven. Plus, there was the time I had to stop to let the chicken cross the road . . .

Just before Cherry Point Road curves to the right, you will notice vines on the right side of the road beyond the deer fence. These are some of the oldest vines of Cherry Point Estate Wines. Turn in at the driveway ahead on the right. The best times to visit Cherry Point are 11:00 AM, 1:00 PM, or 3:00 PM when they host public tours through the vineyard. It's a wonderful way to learn about the history of the area and the farm, and how the grapes grow from bud break to bottle. At time of printing, the new owners, Xavier and Maria Bonilla, were working on a new bistro. As a chef and restaurant owner in West Vancouver, Xavier won a paella contest to rave reviews, so there are good things to come at Cherry Point.

Departing the Cherry Point winery, turn to the right up Cherry Point Road. At the stop sign, turn left on Telegraph Road and right on Fisher Road. Turn right at the light to get back onto Highway 1. Follow the highway through the next set of lights and stay in the righthand lane. You will soon see a sign to turn right for Venturi-Schulze Vineyards. You are essentially doing a U-turn to the driveway, which will now be on your left. Aside from their lovely wines, you can complete your tasting with my favourite beverage in the universe! The Brandenburg No. 3 is an amber dessert wine with beautiful flavour. Michelle Schulze holds down the fort in the weekend tasting room and can tell you the heartfelt story of the No. 3's creation by her stepfather, Giordano Venturi. Michelle's mother, Marilyn Venturi is the third of the trio who run the vineyard and winery with precision and expertise. They take their business seriously and it shows in the products they create. Finish with a taste of Giordano's balsamic vinegar, made in the traditional way. (Giordano is from Modena, don't you know.)

Continue along Highway 1 away from Victoria. At the lights, turn left at

Koksilah Road then take your first left onto Hillbank Road. At the stop sign, turn right on Lakeside Road. Blue Grouse Vineyards is—of course—at the end of Blue Grouse Road, which will sneak up on your left.

The small tasting room overlooks the vineyard and is one of my favourite views in the Cowichan Valley. I like to end the day at Blue Grouse because the vineyard looks stunning as the sun goes down and it's a wonderful place to enjoy the last few sips of wine on your tour. Blue Grouse reds are particularly good, my favourite being the Pinot Noir. Winemaker Hans Kiltz is a perfectionist with his clear, crisp whites and luscious reds. His science background shows in his winemaking. Ask him about treating elephants in Africa. (Well, that's what a large-animal veterinarian does.)

Now perhaps you can see why you can only do so many wineries in a day. If you're up for more, spend the night overlooking Cowichan Bay from the Oceanfront Grand Resort and Marina back in the old fishing village. This casual hotel has brilliant views of the bay. If you prefer bed-and-breakfast, just next door is Dream Weaver B&B. Dine at The Masthead Restaurant in the evening in its nautical setting looking over the water. They have a delicious menu of seafood, Cowichan Bay Farm duck, local venison, and more. I always seem to order a bottle of Alderlea Vineyards red when I'm at The Masthead. Alderlea is north of Duncan and only sporadically open to the public; their wine sells out quickly and isn't available at many restaurants. And, oh, that duck! Have a bottle of the Alderlea Reserve Pinot Noir and the duck with cranberry, thyme, and orange bread pudding and caramelized shallots. I love the Pinot Noir reserve, but maybe the Starling Lane Marechal Foch is a better pairing. These red wines are very different from one another, with the Foch being bigger and bolder. Such a difficult decision when there is such a great island wine list. Now waddle on back to the hotel. Good thing your bed will be close.

The Cowichan Valley really does deserve another day of tasting. After a bite at True Grain Bread, drive through the village and away from Victoria toward the town of Duncan. You will see a sign indicating the way to Highway 1 at which you will turn left and then right again onto the highway. Drive through Duncan and turn left at the lights where the signs indicate to Lake Cowichan, Highway 18.

One of the pleasures of touring the Vancouver Island and Gulf Island wine region is visiting friendly tasting rooms to try wines available for sampling.

Look for an Averill Creek Vineyard highway sign and take the first right after you see it (across from the golf course). Follow the signs up to the winery.

This modern building is one of a kind in the Cowichan Valley. Sip in the tasting room or enjoy a glass on the patio. Dr. Andy Johnston and his wife and partner, Wendy, create some wonderful wines, including an interesting rosé. Their patio is a great spot for a picnic. (Did you stock up at Hilary's?)

Driving back through Duncan toward Victoria, turn right at Miller Road en route to Vigneti Zanatta winery and vineyards. As Miller Road seems to end, turn to the right and then take a quick left, which lands you again on Miller Road. Turn left at Glenora Road and look for signs for Alderlea Farm (no relation to Alderlea Vineyard). Just being built in their new barn, a café is on the rise at this organic and biodynamic farm run by John and Katy Ehrlich and their family.

Farther down Glenora Road, you will see Vigneti Zanatta on your left when you're at the four-way stop, one of the original island wineries. Their Damasco white wine is one of my top summer sippers with its slight effervescence and fruity bouquet. (Tucked away in this neighbourhood, up the road past Zanatta's, is another winery, Godfrey-Brownell.)

Reverse the way you came—up Glenora Road then right on Miller Road. Take a quick right at the perceived end of Miller Road and then left back onto the continuation of Miller Road. Turn right at the stop sign and you're back on Highway 1. The Glenora area of the Cowichan Valley is a bit of a maze.

It would be a shame to spend time in the Cowichan Valley and miss my very favourite dinner spot. Near Shawnigan Lake, Amusé Bistro will break up the drive back to the city and you will be pleasantly surprised by the outstanding cuisine in this modest bistro. It's easy to drive by the small house on the right side of Shawnigan-Mill Bay Road: if you arrive at the four-way stop in Shawnigan Lake, you've gone too far. Spin on your wheels and turn left into the driveway where you will find parking in the back. Notice the garden boxes behind Bradford Boisvert and Leah Bellerive's home. If you dine out back you're bound to see the kitchen staff in their chef whites harvesting from the garden in the middle of dinner. Bellerive and Boisvert have passion for their work, and their love of food and wine is evident in their creative menu. The French-influenced cuisine is continually changing with the seasons. Chef Boisvert's combinations of fresh and local ingredients are both skilled and artistic, with hors d'oeuvres such as *assiette de charcuterie*, *fruits de mer*, or a local cheese plate. My pick, when it's available, is their housemade venison carpaccio. Entrées of seafood, poultry, game, and meat may include confit of smoked pork, grilled lamb, wild salmon, or sole en papillote, always with a delicious accompaniment like potato croquettes or the creamy potato *gratin dauphinois*. Vegetables are flavourful and always fresh. This is a dining experience not to be missed. Amusé Bistro really sums up what the Cowichan Valley is all about—delicious, high-quality cuisine and wine created by passionate artisans.

SAANICH PENINSULA & VICTORIA

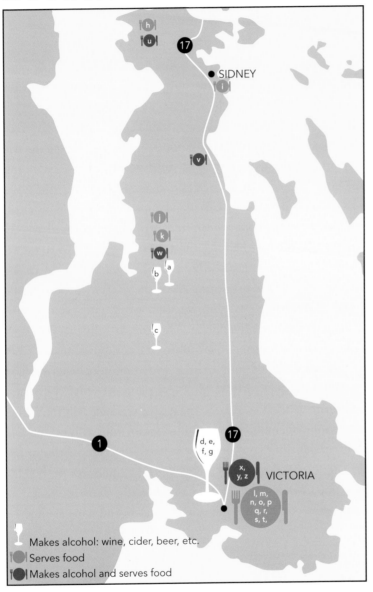

SAANICH PENINSULA

Just a short, 20-minute drive from downtown Victoria, the Saanich Peninsula is perfect for an afternoon tour. If you have a full day, take in the famous Butchart Gardens and enjoy lunch in The Dining Room Restaurant, prepared by Executive Chef Travis Hansen and his culinary team. They take great pride serving all things local, including island wine. Their "Backyard" wine list is, by far, the best selection of island wines available anywhere. It thoughtfully describes each winery, the wine-makers, and the owners, and is a wonderful way to literally taste Vancouver Island.

There are two Peninsula farm-gate wineries that I always enjoy visiting, as well as a distillery and a cidery. If you aren't a lover of cider, you will be! Sea Cider Farm & Ciderhouse, owned by Kristen and Bruce Jordan, has many ciders made from organic apples grown on their farm as well as apples which come from groups like LifeCycles (who pick excess fruit from farms and backyards in the region). Kristen, who once worked across Africa with the United Nations, and Bruce, a lawyer, are proud to be farmers, and they create a warm and hospitable family setting at the relaxed and comfortable ciderhouse. My sweet tooth makes me love the Pomona, which is almost like an icewine. Popular consensus says the Rumrunner is the best, with rich colour and taste, which come from ageing in rum barrels. Kristen brought in old oak barrels, used for Screech, from Newfoundland to age this unique and tasty elixir. A flight of ciders with a cheese and charcuterie plate on the deck overlooking James Island and the mainland mountains is a lovely way to spend the afternoon. On a clear day, you will see Mount Baker.

In the Deep Cove area of the peninsula, Muse Winery offers a wide wine selection of both reds and whites in their tasting room and gift shop. There is also a summertime bistro where you can enjoy a glass or a bottle with a bite to eat, right beside the vineyards. Make sure you read the back labels of their wines. They're a scream!

Starling Lane Winery makes my favourite island white wine, Ortega. You will find Ortega at many island wineries and, in my opinion, it is the epitome of island wine: fresh, crisp, and fruity. Their Marechal Foch is also one of my favourite reds, and a visit to this quaint winery is a must. Each weekend you will be greeted at the gorgeous property by one of the three couples who own Starling Lane. They are always fun for a chat, a slurp, and a sip.

Last but not least on the Saanich Peninsula, stop for a hit of something a little stronger. Victoria Spirits handcrafts an outstanding gin as well as *eau de vie*, and a hemp vodka was released in Spring 2010. Victoria Gin is in great demand and is now available in provincial liquor stores across British Columbia. Even if you're not fond of gin, drop in and give it a try. If you're like me, you'll soon be converted.

A City of Victoria map will assist you to plan your route. I would suggest beginning at Sea Cider Farm & Ciderhouse then continuing in the order written—Muse, Starling Lane, Victoria Sprits. If you're including Butchart Gardens, it would be a good idea to go there before Starling Lane and Victoria Spirits. Or, take in all four tasty spots and then enjoy dinner at Butchart Gardens. If you plan for a Saturday during summer months, you can also include the evening fireworks at Butchart Gardens. This makes for a truly fantastic day!

GULF ISLANDS

The Gulf Islands are home to delightful wineries with ambience and charm.

Ferries depart from the Swartz Bay Terminal regularly for Salt Spring Island's Fulford Harbour. Make sure you arrive at the terminal early if you're visiting on a market Saturday. The ferry ride is just over half an hour and is a beautiful trip. Pick up a Studio Tour Map on the ferry to help guide you to the village of Ganges. Of course, Salt Spring Island is really known for its many artists and studios, but I go for the grub!

If you prefer not to drive, Salt Spring is the best option as they have a public bus service; a bus is always waiting as the ferry docks. You can bus into Ganges and make your way to a winery or two by taxi . . . or hitch-hike, as the locals do!

Salt Spring Island is one of my favourite places to visit, due to the gracious hospitality of the island entrepreneurs and artisans. The best day to visit Salt Spring

GULF ISLANDS

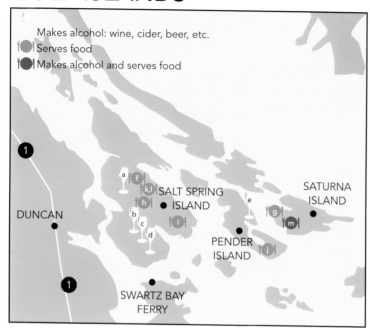

Makes alcohol: wine, cider, beer, etc.
Serves food
Makes alcohol and serves food

DUNCAN
SALT SPRING ISLAND
SATURNA ISLAND
PENDER ISLAND
SWARTZ BAY FERRY

a Mistaken Identity Vineyards (page 107)
b Salt Spring Vineyards (page 75)
c Garry Oaks Winery (page 45)
d Salt Spring Ales
e Morning Bay Vineyard & Estate Winery (page 57)

f Hastings House Country House Hotel (page 220)
g Lighthouse Pub (page 220)
h Foxglove Farm (page 220)
i Salt Spring Island Cheese Company (page 220)
j Poet's Cove Resort & Spa (page 220)
k Salt Spring Island Saturday Market (page 220)
l Bruce's Kitchen (page 220)

m Saturna Island Family Estate Winery (page 81)

is a Saturday from April through October. Salt Spring Island Saturday Market in Ganges, the island's main harbour, is chock-a-block full of fabulous finds and their producers: locally made jewellery and art, coffee roasted on the island, delicious baked items, fabulously fresh produce, and artisan cheese. I always begin by visiting Heather Campbell, better known as The Bread Lady, for a cinnamon bun (if the early birds didn't beat me to it) and to pick up a loaf of wood-fired-oven bread or focaccia. Next, I visit Salt Spring Island Cheese and David Wood, cheesemaker and gourmand, for an oozy and somewhat stinky Blue Juliette plus the hard, aged, sheep-milk Montaña. You can taste all the cheeses. Just try not to buy one of everything! Esteemed farmer and author Michael Ableman is often selling produce from his Foxglove Farm. Between the many vendors you can put together a substantially satisfying picnic. Or pop into Bruce's Kitchen, adjacent to the market, for a fast and fresh lunch that is always tasty.

If you have collected the fixings for a fabulous picnic, I know just the place to enjoy it. The newest winery on Salt Spring, Mistaken Identity, is just up the road from the market. Taste with Sue, the energetic and enchanting wine-shop manager, then grab a bottle and head to the deck. Sit amongst the vines and enjoy.

On your return to the Fulford ferry terminal, you will pass two more wineries. Stop in for a visit at Salt Spring Vineyards where each taste is paired with an island bite. Their vineyard is stunning and the wine shop is always inviting. Garry Oaks Winery is almost next door, down the hill, and offers tastings of their whites and luscious reds.

If you are planning a special weekend, stay and dine at Hastings House, a charming English country resort. The cuisine in their dining room is out of this world. I always have the halibut or Salt Spring Island lamb, and usually have great difficulty deciding, because everything from Chef Marcel Kauer's kitchen is incredible!

Ferries to the other Gulf Islands also depart from the Swartz Bay Terminal north of Victoria. You can island hop if you work with the ferry schedules for a fun weekend getaway.

Pender Island is home to more island vino at Morning Bay Vineyard & Estate Winery. The only winery on Pender, it overlooks the ocean with gorgeous views across the vineyard. Call ahead to book a tour or give them a shout if you want a really special wedding location! The marina down at Poet's Cove Resort and Spa is always alive with summer action. You just may want to spend the weekend.

Saturna Island Family Estate Winery is, naturally, on Saturna Island where you can tour and taste. Saturna makes for a great day trip if you're visiting a few Gulf Islands, and their bistro is a nice spot to take a load off. Or, hang out at the oceanside Saturna Lighthouse Pub and dine from their "better than pub" menu. The pub has been around for more than 30 years and is the most popular spot on Saturna Island.

CENTRAL ISLAND

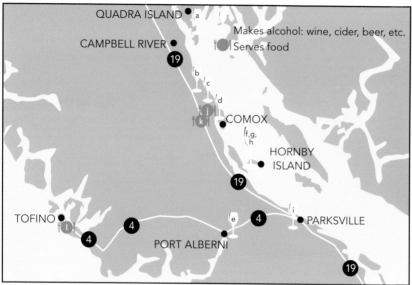

QUADRA ISLAND • a

CAMPBELL RIVER •
19

Makes alcohol: wine, cider, beer, etc.
Serves food

b
c
d
j
k
COMOX
f, g, h

HORNBY ISLAND

19

TOFINO
l
4
4
PORT ALBERNI
e
4
i
PARKSVILLE
19

a SouthEnd Farm Vineyards (page 107)
b Shelter Point Distillery (page 148)
c Beaufort Winery Vineyard & Estate Winery (page 27)
d Surgenor Brewing Company
e Chase & Warren Estate Winery
f Carbrea Vineyards & Winery (page 105)
g Middle Mountain Meadery (page 137)
h Island Spirits Distillery (page 148)
i MooBerry Winery (page 129)

j Atlas Café (page 221)
k Locals (page 221)
l The Pointe Restaurant (page 221)

SIDE TRIPS:
COMOX VALLEY AND SOOKE

Much farther north is the Beaufort winery in the Comox Valley, a three-hour drive from Victoria. This burgeoning foodie paradise is a wonderful destination if you have the time to visit. Do not miss Locals in downtown Courtenay. Chefs Ronald and Tricia St. Pierre are conscientious cooks, neighbours, and friends to their "local" restaurant customers. Hanging on the walls is my idea of true art: pictures and stories about their local suppliers, including farmers, growers, cheesemakers, winemakers, et al. The lunch and dinner menus are as local as you can get and always divine.

SOOKE REGION

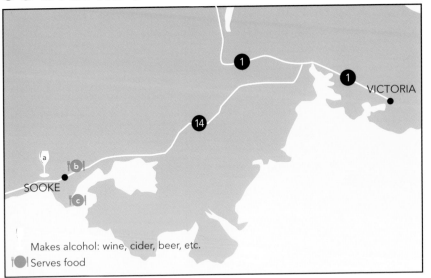

a Tugwell Creek Honey Farm & Meadery (page 137)

b EdGe Restaurant (page 221)
c Sooke Harbour House (page 221)

Along the west coast of Vancouver Island just 45 minutes from Victoria is the famous Sooke Harbour House. Owners Sinclair and Frederique Philip put Vancouver Island on the culinary map when they began serving fresh, local, and seasonal cuisine at their inn long before it became trendy to do so. From the beginning, they have shared their own backyard in a practical and delicious way. Long-time gardener Byron Cook sometimes speaks of the predators in the gardens, including deer and the chefs who are anxious to pick vegetables, herbs, flowers, and more before they are at their peak.

Sooke Harbour House is an incredible dining experience with their hand-printed menu that changes daily. I always opt for the surprise Gastronomic Adventure tasting menu. This multi-course selection of local, organic, seasonal, and wild foods can include wine pairings from their award-winning cellar. After such a fine dinner and fabulous wines, it's a must to stay overnight in one of the uniquely decorated rooms, no two alike. Frederique has a flair for art which is evident both inside Sooke Harbour House and throughout the grounds, right down to the fences. Where else can you stare at a fence as though you were in a museum? All is superior at this world-renowned inn.

When you're in Sooke, visit the Tugwell Creek meadery farther up Sooke Road from the turnoff to Sooke Harbour House. If you've not tasted mead before, this is a unique experience with many flavours, thanks to the bees who produce this intriguing elixir.

In town, a great spot for lunch is EdGe. Named for Edward Tuson, former long-time chef of Sooke Harbour House, and his wife and partner, Gemma Claridge, this hip little spot will knock your socks off. Everything on their chalkboard menu is worth ordering. I dare you to try not to give in to the triangular burger made with beef which Edward grinds himself. This casual stop is a must on a visit to Sooke. Like many of the smaller spots, EdGe is closed Sunday and Monday, so plan ahead or you'll miss out on the most reasonably priced, simple yet gourmet cuisine you've ever had.

Practical Tips

Plan ahead. Know your route and which wineries you will visit.

Call ahead to make sure each destination is open. Most wineries are open April through December but many are open only on weekends.

Keep in mind that it's possible to visit about four wineries in a day.

Be prepared to pay small fees to taste at each winery.

Spit! It's the only way to keep enjoying throughout an entire day of touring.

Please do not drink and drive.

PLANNING YOUR TOUR

COWICHAN TOUR

Alderlea Farm
3390 Glenora Road
Duncan
T: 250-715-0799
W: alderleafarm.com

Cowichan Bay Farm
1560 Cowichan Bay Road
Cowichan Bay
W: cowichanbayfarm.com

Dream Weaver Bed & Breakfast
1682 Botwood Lane
Cowichan Bay
T: 250-748-7688
TF: 1-888-748-7689
W: dreamweaverbedand
breakfast.com

Hilary's Cheese & Deli
1737 Cowichan Bay Road
Cowichan Bay
T: 250-748-5992
W: hilarycheese.com

True Grain Bakery
1725 Cowichan Bay Road
Cowichan Bay
T: 250-746-7664
W: truegrain.ca

Udder Guys
1759 Cowichan Bay Road
Cowichan Valley
T: 250-746-4300
W: udderguysicecream.com

SAANICH

Butchart Gardens: The Dining Room Restaurant
800 Benvenuto Avenue
Brentwood Bay
T: 250-652-8222
W: butchartgardens.com

Haro's at the Sidney Pier Hotel
9805 Seaport Place
Sidney
T: 250-655-9700
W: sidneypier.com

Oceanfront Grand Resort & Marina
1681 Cowichan Bay Road
Cowichan Bay
T: 250-715-1000
W: thegrandresort.com

GULF ISLANDS

Bruce's Kitchen
106-149 Fulford-Ganges Road
Salt Spring Island
T: 250-931-3399
W: bruceskitchen.moonfruit.com

Foxglove Farm
1200 Mount Maxwell Road
Salt Spring Island
T: 250-537-1989
W: foxglovefarmbc.ca

Hastings House Country House Hotel
160 Upper Ganges Road
Salt Spring Island
T: 250-537-2362
W: hastingshouse.com

Poet's Cove Resort and Spa
9801 Spalding Road
South Pender Island
T: 250-629-2100
TF: 1-888-512-7638
W: poetscove.com

Salt Spring Island Cheese
285 Reynolds Road
Salt Spring Island
T: 250-653-2300
W: saltspringcheese.com

Salt Spring Island Saturday Market
Centennial Park in
Ganges Village
Salt Spring Island
T: 250-537-4448

Saturna Lighthouse Pub
100 E Pt Road
Saturna
T: 250-539-5725

RESTAURANTS FEATURING VANCOUVER ISLAND AND GULF ISLAND WINES

Amusé Bistro
1753 Shawnigan-Mill Bay Road
Shawnigan Lake
T: 250-743-3667
W: amusebistro.com

Atlas Café
250 6th Street
Courtenay
T: 250-388-9838
W: atlascafe.ca

Aura Waterfront Restaurant & Patio
680 Montreal Street
Victoria
T: 250-414-6739
W: aurarestaurant.ca

Cafe Brio
944 Fort Street
Victoria
T: 250-383-0009
W: cafe-brio.com

Camille's Fine Westcoast Dining
45 Bastion Square
Victoria
T: 250-381-3433
W: camillesrestaurant.com

Devour
762 Broughton Street
Victoria
T: 250-590-3231
W: devour.ca

EdGe Restaurant
6686 Sooke Road
Sooke
T: 778-425-3343
W: edgerestaurant.ca

Locals
364 8th Street
Courtenay
T: 250-338-6493
W: localscomoxvalley.com

Lure Seafood Restaurant & Bar
45 Songhees Road
Victoria
T: 250-360-5873
W: lurevictoria.com

The Masthead Restaurant
1705 Cowichan Bay Road
Cowichan Bay
T: 250-748-3714
W: themastheadrestaurant.com

The Mark
463 Belleville Street
Victoria
T: 250-380-4487
W: themark.ca

The Pointe Restaurant
500 Osprey Lane
Tofino
T: 250-725-3100
W: wickinn.com

Ristorante La Piola
3189 Quadra Street
Victoria
T: 250-388-4517
W: lapiola.ca

Sips Artisan Bistro
425 Simcoe Street
Victoria
T: 250-590-3519
W: spinnakers.com/sips-artisan-bistro

Sooke Harbour House
1528 Whiffen Spit Road
Sooke
T: 250-642-3421
W: sookeharbourhouse.com

Stage Small Plates Wine Bar
1307 Gladstone Ave
Victoria
T: 250-388-4222
W: stagewinebar.com

CONTRIBUTORS

Long in the tooth and somewhat renowned in the Victoria wine scene over the last 25 years, **Larry Arnold** has toiled in the trenches as a senior product consultant for the BC Liquor Distribution Branch and today spends his time as a writer, wine reviewer, wine judge, educator, and general manager and buyer for Spinnakers Spirit Merchants. He also writes the "Liquid Assets" column for *EAT Magazine*.

Jeff Bateman is an award-winning freelance writer, editor, and mead devotee based in Sooke, BC. His work over the past 30 years has appeared in the *Vancouver Sun*, *Western Living*, *Westworld*, *Vancouver Magazine*, the *Calgary Herald,* and numerous other publications.

Gary Hynes is the founder and editor of *EAT*, a magazine that celebrates the food and wine of Vancouver Island and British Columbia. He has been a sommelier, waiter, restaurant owner, innkeeper, and bass player in a rock band. He has also been a contributor to *Western Living*, *Northwest Palate*, *Wine Access*, and *Century Home*, and has written a cookbook, *The Cooper's Inn Cookbook*. He sits on the *EnRoute* magazine's judging panel for Canada's Best New Restaurants. He lives and works in Victoria, BC, with his wife, Cynthia, son, Colin, and dog, Sam.

Kathryn McAree has blended the perfect ingredients to form a successful career of indulgence. Passion for exploration, food expertise, and a splash or two of wine have mixed well to create Travel With Taste, Vancouver Island's premier culinary tour company. With a love of world travel and happiest when up to her elbows in gastronomic wizardry, Kathy was a foodie from a young age. She spent most of her career in hotels and packaged goods before having a "eureka" moment when travelling in Italy. She realized that the bounty of organic farms, vineyards, chee-semakers, wild seafood, et al., that makes Vancouver Island unique would appeal to a kind of globe-trotting, palate-pleased traveller. Kathy now brings the world to feast at the plenteous tables of Vancouver Island, knowing this secret is best when shared with many. Catch Kathy's radio show *In Good Taste* Saturdays from 1:00 to 2:00 PM on CFAX 1070 in Victoria where she shares her favourite foodie friends and finds.

Julie Pegg is currently *EAT Magazine*'s contributing editor. A wine professional with considerable experience in judging and pairing food and wine, she has been writing for the publication for ten years. She was a product consultant for 14 of her 24 years' employment with BCLDB and still keeps her hand in (and elbow firmly bent) at Dundarave Wine Cellars in West Vancouver. Julie is also a keen amateur cook who loves culinary travel. Farmers' markets are her first stop in any city or town.

When other girls were playing with dolls, **Treve Ring** was reading cookbooks. That interest, along with growing up amid the bounty of beautiful Vancouver Island, propelled her into a career celebrating food and wine. Treve is a certified sommelier, wine consultant, writer, and editor, and a member of the Wine Educators Society. In addition to her regular contributions to *EAT Magazine* and being the drink editor of *EAT online*, she has written for other publications throughout the Pacific Northwest including *Metro Vancouver, Cityfood, BC Wine Trails, Wine Islands, Focus,* and *Visitor's Choice.* She has worked for the BC Restaurant and Foodservices Association, and as catering manager at Swans Hotel, and has managed a season at Marley Farm Winery. In 2007, Treve was invited to be a judge at Oregon's

Northwest Wine Summit, and was also awarded a Les Dames d'Escoffier scholarship for her wine writing and studies. She is currently communications manager and company sommelier for Edible British Columbia.

Adem Tepedelen is a Victoria-based freelance writer and editor who specializes in music, travel, food, and drink. In 2008, he won the Michael Jackson Beer Journalism Award. His work has appeared in *EAT Magazine, Fine Cooking, Wine X, Northwest Palate, Imbibe, All About Beer,* and *CityFood.* He also writes a monthly beer column for *Decibel* magazine called "Brewtal Truth" and does a blog with the same name.

Having lived on the west coast all her life, **Rebecca Wellman** made the move from Vancouver to Vancouver Island in 2004 to pursue her love of fine food and expressive portraiture. A food and lifestyle photographer, her work can be defined as capturing the heart of the person (or the artichoke) with creative passion. Rebecca reads cookbooks like novels, is currently obsessed with dried black mission figs and looks forward to the day when she has enough time to make her own cheese. Rebecca has been a contributor to *EAT Magazine* since 2007. Her work can be viewed at rwellmanphotography.com.

INDEX

Notes